APPLE iPAD

USER GUIDE

The Complete Illustrated, Practical Guide to
Maximizing Your Apple iPad Mini 5

Daniel Smith

i

Contents

Chapter 3

Chapter 4

Chapter 5

Chapter 6

Chapter 7

Chapter 8

Introduction

The iPad mini 2019 is Apple's most totable iPad, and it's deceptively powerful for its small size. It has a bright 7.9-inch display that works with the Apple Pencil and a chipset that smokes the small tablet competition.

It's Apple's most satisfyingly totable iPad and proof that things won't change very much when serious small tablet competition is nowhere to be found in 2020.

The familiar 7.9-inch display feels perfectly sized to grip in one hand and operate with two, just as it did when the iPad mini 4 released nearly four years ago. Almost nothing has improved on the outside.

Beneath the bright display, however, Apple tweaked the iPad mini 2019 to work with the first-generation Apple Pencil. It's so easy to quickly pick up this tablet, flick open the Smart Cover and instantly scribble some notes. It's portable and carefree to use and then simply toss in a bag. Here is our user guide to help you maximize your iPad Mini 5 to the fullest.

Chapter 1

Get started

Turn on and set up iPad

Turn on and set up your new iPad over an Internet connection. You can also set up an iPad by connecting it to your computer. If you have another iPhone, iPad, iPod touch, or an Android device, you can transfer your data to your new iPad.

Prepare for setup

To make setup as smooth as possible, have the following items available:

- An Internet connection through a Wi-Fi network (you may need the name and password of the network) or cellular data service through a carrier (Wi-Fi + Cellular models)

- Your Apple ID and password; if you don't have an Apple ID, you can create one during setup

- Your credit or debit card account information, if you want to add a card to Apple Pay during setup

- Your previous iPad or a backup of your device, if you're transferring your data to your new device

- Your Android device, if you're transferring your Android content

Turn on and set up your iPad

- Press and hold the top button until the Apple logo appears.

- If iPad doesn't turn on, you might need to charge the battery.

Do one of the following:

- Tap Set Up Manually, then follow the onscreen setup instructions.

- If you have another iPhone, iPad, or iPod touch with iOS 11, iPadOS 13, or later, you can use Quick Start to automatically set up your new device. Bring the two devices close together, then follow the onscreen instructions to securely copy many of your settings, preferences, and iCloud Keychain. You can then restore the rest of your data and content to your new device from your iCloud backup.

- Or, if both devices have iOS 12.4, iPadOS 13, or later, you can transfer all your data wirelessly from your previous device to your new one. Keep your devices near each other and plugged into power until the migration process is complete.

- You can also transfer your data using a wired connection between your devices.

- If you're blind or have low vision, triple-click the Home button to turn on VoiceOver, the screen reader.

Set up cellular service on iPad (Wi-Fi + Cellular models)

If you have a Wi-Fi + Cellular model, you can sign up for a cellular data plan. This helps you stay connected to the Internet when you're away from a Wi-Fi network. You can set up a cellular data plan with any of the following:

- eSIM

- Embedded Apple SIM or Apple SIM card

- Third-party nano-SIM (from a cellular provider)

Set up your cellular plan with eSIM

On models that support eSIM, you can activate the cellular service from your iPad. You may also be able to travel abroad with iPad and sign up for cellular service with a local carrier in the region you're visiting. This isn't available in all regions, and not all carriers are supported. Go to Settings > Cellular Data.

Do one of the following:

- To set up the first cellular plan on your iPad, select a carrier, then follow the onscreen instructions.

- To add another cellular plan to your iPad, tap Add a New Plan.

- To scan a QR code provided by your carrier, tap Other. Position iPad so that the QR code provided by your carrier appears in the frame, or enter the details manually. You may be asked to enter a confirmation code provided by your carrier.

Alternatively, you can activate your cellular plan through your carrier's app (if supported). Go to the App Store, download your carrier's app, then use the app to purchase a cellular plan.

You can store more than one eSIM on your iPad, but you can use only one eSIM at a time. To switch eSIMs, go to Settings > Cellular Data, then tap the plan you want to use (below Cellular Plans).

Set up your cellular plan with an embedded Apple SIM or Apple SIM card

On models with an embedded Apple SIM or Apple SIM card, you can activate the cellular service from your iPad. You may also be able to travel abroad with iPad and sign up for cellular service with a local carrier in the region you're visiting. This isn't available in all regions, and not all carriers are supported. Go to Settings > Cellular Data.

- Tap Add a New Plan, then follow the onscreen instructions. You can choose a carrier and a plan, or you can add your iPad to an existing plan.

Install a nano-SIM

You can install an Apple SIM card or a nano-SIM provided by a carrier.

- Insert a paper clip or SIM eject tool (not included) into the small hole of the SIM tray, then push in toward iPad to eject the tray.

- Remove the tray from iPad.

- Place the nano-SIM in the tray. The angled corner determines the correct orientation.

- Insert the tray back into iPad.

- If you previously set up a PIN on the nano-SIM, carefully enter the PIN when prompted.

WARNING: Never try to guess a SIM PIN. An incorrect guess can permanently lock your SIM, and you won't be able to use cellular data through your carrier until you get a new SIM.

Cellular data requires a wireless data plan. If you're using a third-party nano-SIM, contact your carrier to set up service.

Manage your cellular data service

Go to Settings > Cellular Data. Do any of the following:

- Restrict all data to Wi-Fi: Turn off Cellular Data.

- Turn on or off LTE and roaming: Tap Cellular Data Options.

- Turn on Personal Hotspot: Tap Set Up Personal Hotspot (available from certain carriers), then follow the onscreen instructions.

- Manage your cellular account: Tap Manage [account name] or Carrier Services.

Manage Apple ID and iCloud settings on iPad

Your Apple ID is the account you use to access Apple services such as the App Store, the iTunes Store,

8

Apple Books, Apple Music, FaceTime, iCloud, iMessage, and more.

Use iCloud to securely store your photos, videos, documents, music, apps, and more—and keep them updated across all your devices. With iCloud, you can easily share photos, calendars, locations, and more with friends and family. You can even use iCloud to help you find your iPad if you lose it.

iCloud provides you with a free email account and 5 GB of storage for your mail, documents, photos and videos, and backups. Your purchased music, apps, TV shows, and books don't count against your available storage space. You can upgrade your iCloud storage right from iPad.

Note: Some iCloud features have minimum system requirements. The availability of iCloud and its features varies by country or region.

Sign in with your Apple ID

If you didn't sign in during setup, do the following:

- Go to Settings .

- Tap Sign in to your iPad.

- Enter your Apple ID and password.

- If you don't have an Apple ID, you can create one.

- If you protect your account with two-factor authentication,   enter   the   six-digit verification code.

Change your Apple ID settings

Go to Settings > [your name]. Do any of the following:

- Update your contact information

- Change your password

- Manage Family Sharing

Change your iCloud settings

- Go to Settings > [your name] > iCloud.

Do any of the following:

- See your iCloud storage status.

- Upgrade   your   iCloud   storage—tap   Manage Storage > Change Storage Plan.

- Turn on the features you want to use, such as Photos, Mail, Contacts, and Messages.

Move content manually from your Android device to your iOS device

Here are some tips for transferring your contacts, photos, music, documents, and more from your Android device to your new iPhone, iPad, or iPod touch.

You can also use the Move to iOS app to automatically transfer your Android content to your new iOS device. If you can't use the app, you can move your content manually instead.

Mail, contacts, and calendars

iOS works with email providers like Google, Microsoft Exchange, Yahoo, and more, so you can probably keep the email, contacts, and calendars that you have now. To get started, add each of your email accounts to your iPhone. Then go to Settings > Passwords & Accounts.

Photos and videos

To move photos and videos from your Android device to your iOS device, use a computer with iTunes:

- Connect your Android to your computer and find your photos and videos. On most devices, you can find these files in DCIM > Camera. On a Mac, install Android File Transfer, open it, then go to DCIM > Camera.

- Choose the photos and videos that you want to move and drag them to a folder on your computer.

- Disconnect your Android and connect your iPhone to your computer.

- Open iTunes on your computer and sync your Photos to your iPhone. You can find your photos and videos on your iPhone in Photos > Albums.

You can also use iCloud Photos to keep your photos and videos in iCloud, so you can access your library from any device, anytime you want.

Music

When you switch to iPhone, you can bring your music with you. Just use a computer with iTunes to transfer the music. If you use a streaming music app, go to the App Store, get the app, then sign in with your user name and password. If you use Apple Music, just sign in on your iOS device.

To move music from your Android device to your iOS device, use a computer with iTunes:

- Connect your Android device to your computer and find your music. On most devices, you can find these files in Music. On a Mac, install Android File Transfer, open it, then go to Music.

- Select the songs that you want to move and drag them to a folder on your computer.

- Disconnect your Android device and connect your iPhone to your computer.

- Open iTunes on your computer, go to your Library, and click Music.

- Open the folder where you put your songs and drag them to the Music view in iTunes.

- Select your iOS device and click Music. You can choose to sync your entire library or select only the songs or artists that you just added

- Click Sync. You can find your music on your iPhone in the Music app.

Books and PDFs

To move eBooks from your Android device, you can either import them to your iOS device or access them through apps like Kindle, Nook, Google Play Books, and others. To access books from an app, go to the App Store, get the app, then sign in with your username and password.

To move ePub books and PDFs from your Android to your iOS device, use a computer with iTunes:

- Connect your Android device to your computer and find your books and PDFs. On most devices, you can find these files in Documents. On a Mac, install Android File Transfer, open it, then go to Documents.

- Select the books and PDFs that you want to move and drag them to a folder on your computer.

- Disconnect your Android device and connect your iPhone to your computer.

- Drag the books and PDFs into your library. On a Mac, go to Books > List, and drag your books there. On a PC, go to iTunes > Books.

- Open iTunes on your computer and sync your ePub books and PDFs. You can find your ePub books and PDFs on your iPhone inBooks > All Books.

Documents

If you store documents in the cloud or another service like Dropbox, Google Drive, or Microsoft OneDrive, you can download the app from the App Store, then sign in. You can also bring all your files together with the Files app.

Whether your files are on your iOS device, in iCloud Drive, or on another service like Dropbox or Box, you can easily browse, search, and organize your files all in one place.

The iOS apps for Pages, Numbers, and Keynote work with several file types, including Microsoft Office documents. If you don't use the cloud to transfer your documents, get the apps:

- Go to the App Store on your iPhone and install Pages, Numbers, and Keynote.

- Connect your Android to your computer and find your documents. On most devices, you can find these files in Documents. On a Mac, install Android File Transfer, open it, then go to Documents.

- Select the documents that you want to move and drag them to a folder on your computer.

- Open iTunes on your computer and sync your documents to your iOS device.

Apps

Most apps that you use on your Android device are available in the App Store. Go to the App Store, search for the apps that you have now, and install them.

How to download iPadOS on an Apple tablet

iPadOS represents a bit of a shift for Apple, as it continues to differentiate how the operating system on the iPad works, feels, and functions. Now, iPadOS is available to the public, bringing with it a number of great features, including mouse support, a revamped home screen, and more.

There are plenty of features to check out, but to see them for yourself you'll need to update your iPad. Here's how to download iPadOS.

Compatible devices

Before installing iPadOS, you'll need to make sure your iPad is compatible with the new operating system. Apple is known for supporting devices for a long time, but some older models won't get the update, so it's worth checking the list below to see if your iPad will get support.

- iPad Air 2 and 3

- iPad Mini 4 and 5

- iPad (6th and 7th generations)

- 9.7-inch iPad Pro

- 10.5-inch iPad Pro

- 11-inch iPad Pro

- 12.9-inch iPad Pro

Installing iPadOS onto your device is really super simple. Here's how to get iPadOS on your iPad. Note, if you think you might not like iPadOS and might want to roll back to iOS 12, then it's worth creating a backup before you start. Check out the instructions below on creating a backup.

- Open the Settings app.

- Head to General > Software Update.

- Your iPad will check for updates and you should get a notification telling you that iPadOS is ready to install. Tap Download and Install.

- It may take a few minutes to download and install the update, and you won't be able to use your iPad during the update process.

Back up your iPad

Think you might want to roll back to iOS 12 after updating your device? In that case, you should make a backup before upgrading. There are two ways to backup your iPad — using iCloud, or through iTunes.

Backing up using iCloud

Backing up your iPad using iCloud is the easiest method. Here's how to do it for yourself.

- Make sure you're connected to a Wi-Fi network.

- Open the Settings app, press your name, then tap iCloud.

- Scroll down to iCloud Backup, then tap Back Up Now.

If you're unsure as to whether the backup is complete, you can head to Settings, then tap iCloud > iCloud Storage > Manage Storage, then tap on the device on the list.

Backing up on a Mac running MacOS Catalina

MacOS Catalina no longer has iTunes, so backing up your device on a Mac is a little different than it used to be. If you're running MacOS Catalina, you'll instead use the Finder app. Here's how it's done.

- Connect your iPad to your Mac.

- Follow the onscreen instructions — you may need to enter a PIN code or tap Trust This Computer.

- Open the Finder app and select your iPad in the sidebar.

- Press the General tab, then tap Back Up Now to manually back up your iPad.

Backing up on a Mac or PC with iTunes

If you have a Mac with Mojave or older, or a PC with iTunes, then you'll use iTunes to back up your iPad. Here's how to do it.

- Make sure you have the latest version of iTunes, then connect your iPad.

- Follow the onscreen instructions — you may need to enter a PIN code or tap Trust This Computer.

- Open iTunes and select your iPad.

- Press the Back Up Now button to save your data.

Rolling back from iPadOS to iOS 12

If you created a backup of your device before upgrading to iPadOS, you can downgrade back to iOS 12. Here's how to roll back from iPadOS to iOS 12.

- To downgrade to iOS 12, you'll need to put your iPad into recovery mode.

- On an iPad with Face ID, hold the top button and either volume button until you see the Recovery Mode icon. On an iPad with a Home button, hold the side or top button until you see it.

- Plug your iPad into your computer using the cable that came with it.

- On the iTunes popup, click the Restore button.

- Click Restore and Update to confirm.

- An iOS 12 updater should appear. Press Next.

- Click Agree to accept the Terms and Conditions.

- Once the updater is finished, you'll have a clean install of iOS 12 on your device. You'll need to restore from your iCloud or iTunes backups to get your data back.

- Follow the instructions below depending on the type of backup you made.

Restore from an iCloud backup

Here's how to restore your device from an iCloud backup from before you updated to iOS 12.

- On the Apps & Data screen, tap Restore from iCloud Backup and sign in to iCloud.

- Tap Choose Backup and choose the backup you made before installing iPadOS.

- Make sure you select the right backup — if you've had your device for more than a day, you may have another backup from when you were already on iPadOS.

Restore from an iTunes backup

Did you make an iTunes backup instead? Here's how to restore from an iTunes backup.

- Tap Restore from iTunes Backup on the Apps & Data screen.

- Open iTunes on your computer, make sure your device is connected through a cable, then tap Trust This Computer.

- Select your device in iTunes, then press Summary and hit the Restore Backup button.

- Pick the backup from when your device was still running iOS 12.

- Keep your iPad connected to your computer until after it finishes syncing.

Chapter 2

Basic Guide:

Wake and unlock iPad

iPad turns off the display to save power, locks for security, and goes to sleep when you're not using it. You can quickly wake and unlock iPad when you want to use it again. To wake iPad, do one of the following:

• Press the top button.

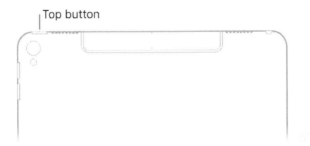

Top button

• Tap the screen. Or, on **supported models**, you can tap the screen with Apple Pencil to wake iPad and open Notes.

Unlock iPad with Face ID

1. On **supported models**, tap the screen, then glance at your iPad. The lock icon animates from closed to open to indicate that iPad is unlocked.

2. Swipe up from the bottom of the screen to view the Home screen.

To lock iPad again, press the top button. iPad locks automatically if you don't touch the screen for a minute or so. However, if Attention Aware Features is turned on in Settings ⚙ > Face ID & Passcode, iPad won't dim or lock as long as it detects attention.

Unlock iPad with Touch ID

On **supported models**, press the Home button using the finger you registered with Touch ID.

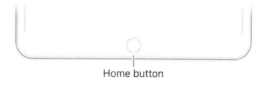

Home button

To lock iPad again, press the top button. iPad locks automatically if you don't touch the screen for a minute or so.

Unlock iPad with a passcode

25

1. Swipe up from the bottom of the Lock screen or press the Home button.

2. Enter the passcode (if you set up iPad to require a passcode).

To lock iPad again, press the top button. iPad locks automatically if you don't touch the screen for a minute or so.

View previews and quick actions menus on iPad

On the **Home** screen, in **Control Center**, and in apps, you can see previews, open quick actions menus, and more.

- In **Photos**, touch and hold an image to preview it and see a list of options.

- In **Mail**, touch and hold a message in a mailbox to preview the message contents and see a list of options.

- On the Home screen, touch and hold an app icon briefly to open a quick actions menu. If the icons start to jiggle, tap **Done** at the top right or press the **Home button** (models with a Home button), then try again.

- Open Control Center, then touch and hold an item like Camera or the brightness control to see options.

- On the Lock screen, touch and hold a notification briefly to respond to it.

- When typing, touch and hold the Space bar with one finger to turn your keyboard into a trackpad.

Explore the iPad Home screen and open apps

Get to know the Home screen and apps on your iPad. The Home screen shows all your apps organized into pages. More pages are added when you need space for apps.

1. To go to the Home screen, swipe up from the bottom edge of the screen or press the Home button.

2. Swipe left or right to browse apps on other Home screen pages.

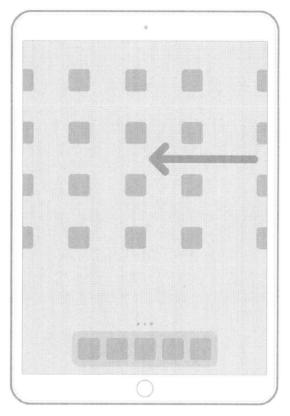

3. To open an app, tap its icon on the Home screen.

4. To return to the first Home screen page, swipe up from the bottom edge of the screen or press the Home button.

Change common iPad settings

Use Settings (located on the Home screen) to configure and customize your iPad settings. You can set your language and region, change the name of your iPad, choose different sounds for notifications, and much more.

The settings for specific apps are explained in the chapters for those apps. The following sections give some examples of common settings, including how to find them.

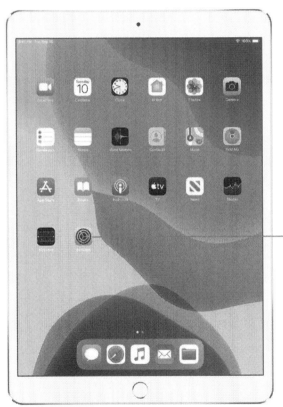

Tap Settings to change iPad settings (volume, display brightness, and more).

Find settings

Go to Settings ⚙, swipe down from the left side of the screento reveal the search field, enter a term—"iCloud," for example—then tap a setting on the left side of the screen.

Set the date and time

By default, the date and time, visible on the Lock screen, are set automatically based on your location. If they're incorrect, you can adjust them.

1. Go to Settings > General > Date & Time.

2. Turn on either of the following:

   - **Set Automatically**: iPad gets the correct time over the network and updates it for the time zone you're in. Some networks don't support network time, so in some regions iPad may not be able to automatically determine the local time.

   - **24-Hour Time**: (not available in all regions) iPad displays the hours from 0 to 23.

To change the default date and time, turn off Set Automatically, then change the date and time displayed.

Set the language and region

1. Go to Settings > General > Language & Region.

2. Set the following:

   - The language for iPad

   - The region

- The calendar format

- The temperature unit (Celsius or Fahrenheit)

To add a keyboard for another language, go to Settings > General > Keyboard > Keyboards, then tap Add New Keyboard.

Change the name of your iPad

The name of your iPad is used by iCloud, AirDrop, your Personal Hotspot, and your computer.

1. Go to Settings ⚙ > General > About > Name.

2. Tap ⊗, enter a new name, then tap Done.

Set up mail, contacts, and calendar accounts

In addition to the apps that come with iPad and that you use with iCloud, iPad works with Microsoft Exchange and many of the most popular Internet-based mail, contacts, and calendar services.

1. Go to Settings ⚙ > Passwords & Accounts > Add Account.

2. To add a mail account, tap an email service—for example, Google, Yahoo, or Aol.com—then enter your email account information.

3. To add a contacts or calendar account, tap Other, then do any of the following:

- Contacts using an LDAP or CardDAV account, if your company or organization supports it.

- Calendars using a CalDAV calendar account; you can also subscribe to iCalendar (.ics) calendars or import them from Mail.

- *Add a contacts account:* Tap Add LDAP Account or Add CardDAV Account (if your company or organization supports it), then enter your information.

- *Add a calendar account:* Tap Add CalDAV Account, then enter your information.

- *Subscribe to iCal (.ics) calendars:* Tap Add Subscribed Calendar, then enter the URL of the .ics file to subscribe to; or import an .ics file from Mail.

  Change or lock the screen orientation on iPad.

  Many apps give you a different view when you rotate iPad.

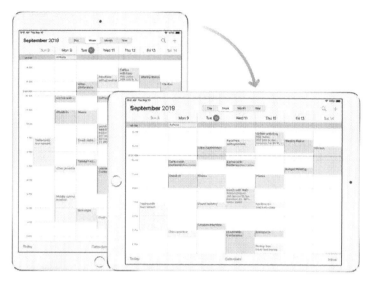

Lock or unlock the screen orientation

You can lock the screen orientation so that it doesn't change when you rotate iPad.

Open Control Center, then tap 🔄.

When the screen orientation is locked, 🔒 appears in the status bar.

Change the wallpaper on iPad

On iPad, choose an image or photo as wallpaper for the Lock screen or Home screen. You can choose from dynamic and still images.

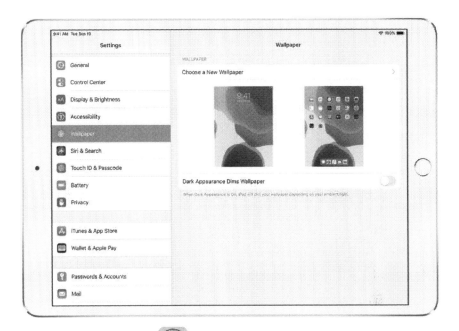

1. Go to Settings > Wallpaper > Choose a New Wallpaper.

2. Do one of the following:

   • Choose a preset image from a group at the top of the screen (Dynamic, Stills, and so on).

   Wallpaper marked with ◉ changes appearance when Dark Mode is turned on.

   • Select one of your own photos (tap an album, then tap the photo).

36

To reposition your selected image, pinch open to zoom in on it, then drag the image to move it. Pinch closed to zoom back out.

Tap Set, then choose one of the following:

- Set Lock Screen

- Set Home Screen

- Set Both

You may be able to make your wallpaper move when you change the viewing angle of your screen by turning on Perspective Zoom when you choose new wallpaper. To turn on the Perspective Zoom option for wallpaper you've already set, go to Settings > Wallpaper, tap the image of the Lock screen or Home screen, then tap Perspective.

Note: The Perspective Zoom option doesn't appear for all wallpaper choices, and it doesn't appear if Reduce Motion (in Accessibility settings) is turned on.

Adjust the iPad screen brightness and color

On iPad, dim the screen to extend battery life, set Dark Mode, and use Night Shift. On supported models, use True Tone to automatically adapt the color and intensity of the display to match the light in your environment.

Turn Dark Mode on or off

Dark Mode gives the entire iPad experience a dark color scheme that's perfect for low-light environments. You can turn on Dark Mode from Control Center or set it to turn on automatically at night (or on a custom schedule) in Settings. With Dark Mode turned on, you can use your iPad while, for example, reading in bed, without disturbing the person next to you.

Do any of the following:

- Open Control Center, touch and hold ☼, then tap ◐ to turn Dark Mode on or off.

- Go to Settings ⚙ > Display & Brightness, then select Dark to turn on Dark Mode or select Light to turn it off.

Schedule Dark Mode to turn on and off automatically

1. Go to Settings ⚙ > Display & Brightness.

2. Turn on Automatic, then tap Options.

3. Select either Sunset to Sunrise or Custom Schedule.

   If you choose Custom Schedule, tap the options to schedule the times you want Dark Mode to turn on and off.

If you select Sunset to Sunrise, iPad uses the data from your clock and geo-location to determine when it's nighttime for you.

Adjust the screen brightness manually

To make your iPad screen dimmer or brighter, do one of the following:

- Open Control Center, then drag ☼.

- Go to Settings ⚙ > Display & Brightness, then drag the slider.

Adjust the screen brightness automatically

iPad adjusts the screen brightness for current light conditions using the built-in ambient light sensor.

1. Go to Settings ⚙ > Accessibility.

2. Tap Display & Text Size, then turn on Auto-Brightness.

Turn True Tone on or off

On supported models, turn on True Tone to automatically adapt the color and intensity of the display to match the light in your environment. Do any of the following:

- Open Control Center, touch and hold ☼, then tap ☀ to turn True Tone on or off.

- Go to Settings ◉ > Display & Brightness, then turn True Tone on or off.

Turn Night Shift on or off

You can turn on Night Shift manually, which is helpful when you're in a darkened room during the day.

- Open Control Center, touch and hold ☼, then tap ☾.

Schedule Night Shift to turn on and off automatically

Use Night Shift to shift the colors in your display to the warmer end of the spectrum at night and make viewing the screen easier on your eyes.

1. Go to Settings ◉ > **Display & Brightness > Night Shift.**

2. Turn on **Scheduled**.

3. To adjust the color balance for **Night Shift**, drag the slider below Color Temperature toward the warmer or cooler end of the spectrum.

4. Tap **From**, then select either **Sunset** to **Sunrise** or **Custom Schedule**.

   If you choose Custom Schedule, tap the options to schedule the times you want Night Shift to turn on and off.

   If you select Sunset to Sunrise, iPad uses the data from your clock and geo-location to determine when it's nighttime for you.

   Note: The Sunset to Sunrise option isn't available if you turned off Location Services in Settings ◉ > Privacy, or if you turned off Setting Time Zone in Settings ◉ > Privacy > Location Services > System Services.

   Magnify the iPad screen with Display Zoom

On iPad Pro (12.9-inch), you can magnify the screen display.

1. Go to Settings ◉ > Display & Brightness.

2. Tap View (below Display Zoom), choose Zoomed, then tap Set.

Chapter 3
How to use the Apps

Switch between apps on iPad

Use the Dock, the App Switcher, or a gesture to quickly switch from one app to another on your iPad. When you switch back, you can pick up right where you left off.

Open an app from the dock

From any app, swipe up from the bottom edge of the screen and pause to reveal the Dock, then tap the app you want to use. Favorite apps are on the left side of the Dock, and suggested apps—like the ones you opened recently and ones open on your iPhone or Mac—appear on the right side of the Dock.

Favorite apps   Suggested apps

Use the App Switcher

1. To see all your open apps in the App
Switcher, do one of the following:

- Swipe up from the bottom edge and pause in the
center of the screen.

- Double-click the Home button (models with the
Home button).

2. To browse the open apps, swipe right, then
tap the app or Split View workspace you
want to use.

Switch between open apps

- Swipe left or right with four or five fingers.

- Swipe left or right with one finger along the bottom edge of the screen. (On models with a Home button, perform this gesture with a slight arc.)

To turn off the multi finger swipe gesture, go to Settings ⚙ > General > Multitasking & Dock.

Move and organize apps on iPad

Rearrange the apps on the Home screen, organize them in folders, and move them to other pages (or screens). You can also reorder your pages.

Move apps around the Home screen, into the Dock, or to other pages

1. Touch and hold an app on the Home screen until the app icons jiggle.

2. Drag an app to one of the following locations:

- Another location on the same page

- The Dock at the bottom of the screen

- Another page—drag the app to the right edge of the screen. You might need to wait a second for

46

the new page to appear. The dots above the Dock shows how many pages you have, and which one you're viewing.

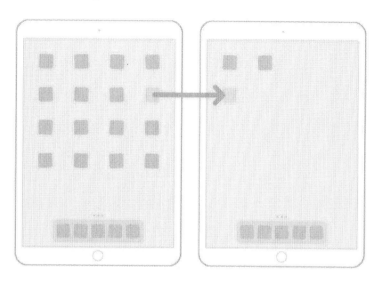

3. When you're done, swipe up   from the bottom edge of the screen or press the Home button (models with the Home button).

Create folders and organize your apps

You can group your apps in folders to help you find them more easily on the Home screen.

1. Touch and hold any app on the screen until the app icons jiggle.

2. To create a folder, drag an app onto another app.

3. Drag other apps into the folder.

4. You can have multiple pages of apps in the folder.

5. To rename the folder, tap the name field, then enter the new name.

6. When you're done, swipe up from the bottom edge of the screen or press the Home button (models with the Home button).

To delete a folder, drag all the apps out of the folder. The folder is automatically deleted.

Reset the Home screen and apps to their original layout

1. Go to Settings 🔘 > General > Reset.

2. Tap Reset Home Screen Layout. Any folders you've created are removed, and apps you've downloaded are alphabetically ordered after apps that came with your iPad.

Remove apps

Remove apps from iPad

You can easily remove apps from your iPad. If you change your mind, you can download the apps again later.

Remove apps from the Home screen

1. Touch and hold any app on the screen until the app icons jiggle.

2. Tap the Close button on the app you want to remove, then tap Delete.

3. When you're done, swipe up from the bottom edge or press the Home button (models with the Home button).

In addition to removing third-party apps, you can remove the following built-in Apple apps that came with your iPad:

- Books

- Calendar

- Contacts (Contact information remains available through Messages, Mail, FaceTime, and other apps. To remove a contact, you must restore Contacts.)

- FaceTime

- Files

- Find My

- Home

- iTunes Store

- Mail

- Maps

- Measure

- Music

- News

- Notes

- Photo Booth

- Podcasts

- Reminders

- Shortcuts

- Stocks

- Tips

- TV

- Voice Memos

Note: When you remove a built-in app from your Home screen, you also remove any related user data and configuration files. Removing built-in apps from your Home screen can affect other system functionality.

Keep your favorite apps readily available on iPad

On iPad, you can keep your favorite apps handy in Control Center or Today View. In Control Center, shortcuts give you quick access to apps like Notes or Voice Memos. In Today View, widgets provide timely information from your favorite apps at a glance.

You can also perform common app functions from the Home screen. On the Home screen, touch and hold an app icon to open a quick actions menu.

Customize Control Center to include your favorite apps

You can add shortcuts to many apps such as Notes, Voice Memos, and more.

1. Go to Settings > Control Center > Customize Controls.

2. Tap the Insert button ⊕ next to each app you want to add.

Add widgets in Today View

1. Get information from your favorite apps at a glance. Choose from Maps Nearby, Calendar, Notes, News, Reminders, and more.

2. From the Home screen, swipe right to open Today View.

3. Scroll to the bottom, then tap Edit.

4. Tap the Insert button ⊕ next to each app you want to add, then tap **Done**.

Perform quick actions from the Home screen

On the Home screen, touch and hold app icons to open quick actions menus.

For example:

- Touch and hold Camera, then choose Take Selfie.

- Touch and hold Maps, then choose Send My Location.

- Touch and hold Notes, then choose New Note.

Note: If you touch and hold an app icon for too long before choosing a quick action, the icons begin to jiggle. Tap **Done** or press the Home button (models with a Home button), then try again.

Draw in apps with Markup on iPad

In supported apps such as Messages, Mail, Notes, and Books, you can annotate photos, screenshots, PDFs, and more using built-in drawing tools.

Show, move, and hide the Markup toolbar

To show the Markup toolbar in a supported app, tap the Markup Switch button off or Markup, then do any of the following:

- Move the Markup toolbar: Drag the toolbar to any edge of the screen.

(Drag from the middle edge of the toolbar closest to the center of the screen.)

- Automatically minimize the toolbar when you're drawing or entering text: Tap the Ellipsis button ⊙, then turn on Auto-minimize.

To show the full toolbar again, tap the minimized version.

- Hide the toolbar: Tap the Markup Switch button on ⊗ or Done.

Draw with Markup

In the Markup toolbar, tap the pen, marker, or pencil tool, then write or draw with your finger or Apple Pencil (supported models).

Note: If you don't see the Markup toolbar on supported app, tap the Markup Switch button off or Markup. If the toolbar is minimized, tap its minimized version.

While drawing, do any of the following:

- Change the line weight: Tap the drawing tool in the toolbar, then choose an option.

- Change the opacity: Tap the drawing tool in the toolbar, then drag the slider.

- Change the color: Choose a color from the color picker in the toolbar.

- Undo a mistake: Tap the Undo button.

- Draw a straight line: Tap the ruler tool in the toolbar, then draw a line along the edge of the ruler.

- To change the angle of the ruler, touch and hold the ruler with two fingers, then rotate your fingers.

- To move the ruler without changing its angle, drag it with one finger.

- To make the ruler disappear, tap the ruler tool again.

Erase a mistake

Tap the eraser tool in the Markup toolbar in a supported app, then do one of the following:

- Erase with the pixel eraser: Scrub over the mistake with your finger or Apple Pencil.

- Erase with the object eraser: Touch the object with your finger or Apple Pencil.

- Switch between the pixel and the object erasers: Tap the eraser tool again, then choose Pixel Eraser or Object Eraser.

Note: If you don't see the Markup toolbar, tap the Markup Switch button off Ⓐ or Markup. If the toolbar is minimized, tap its minimized version.

- Move elements of your drawing

- In the Markup toolbar, tap the lasso tool (between the eraser and ruler tools), then drag around the elements to make a selection.

Note: If you don't see the Markup toolbar in a supported app, tap the Markup Switch button off or Markup. If the toolbar is minimized, tap its minimized version.

Move elements of your drawing

1. In the Markup toolbar, tap the lasso tool (between the eraser and ruler tools), then drag around the elements to make a selection.

2. Lift your finger or Apple Pencil, then drag your selection to a new location.

Tip: You can take a screenshot and immediately begin marking it up with Apple Pencil by swiping up from the bottom-left corner of the screen. To mark up a screenshot right after you take it if you don't have Apple Pencil, tap the thumbnail that appears for a few moments in the bottom-left corner of the screen.

Add text, shapes, and signatures with Markup on iPad

In supported apps, you can use Markup to add text, speech bubbles, shapes, and signatures.

Add text

1. In the Markup toolbar in a supported app, tap the Add Annotation button $\oplus$, then tap Text.

   Note: If you don't see the Markup toolbar, tap the Markup Switch button off $\oslash$ or Markup. If the toolbar is minimized, tap its minimized version.

2. Double-tap the text box.

3. Use the keyboard to enter text.

To change text after you add it, tap the text to select it, then do any of the following:

- Change the font, size, or layout: Tap the Shape Attributes button ᴀA in the toolbar, then choose an option.

- Delete, edit, or duplicate the text: Tap Edit, then choose an option.

- Move the text: Drag it.

To hide the Markup toolbar when you finish, tap the Markup Switch button on Ⓐ or Done.

Add a shape

1. In the Markup toolbar in a supported app, tap the Add Annotation button , then choose a shape.

   Note: If you don't see the Markup toolbar, tap the Markup Switch button off or Markup. If the toolbar is minimized, tap its minimized version.

To adjust the shape, do any of the following:

- Move the shape: Drag it.

- Resize the shape: Drag any blue dot along the shape's outline.

- Change the outline color: Tap a color in the color picker.

- Fill the shape with color or change the line thickness: Tap the Shapes Attribute button 🖿, then choose an option.

- Adjust the form of an arrow or speech bubble shape: Drag a green dot.

- Delete or duplicate a shape: Tap it, then choose an option.

- To hide the Markup toolbar when you finish, tap the Markup Switch button on or **Done**.

Add your signature

In the Markup toolbar in a supported app, tap the Add Annotation button, then choose Signature.

Note: If you don't see the Markup toolbar, tap the Markup Switch button off or Markup. If the toolbar is minimized, tap its minimized version.

To hide the Markup toolbar when you finish, tap the Markup Switch button on or Done.

Zoom in or magnify in Markup on iPad

In Markup on supported apps, zoom in to draw the details. Use the magnifier when you only need to see the details.

Zoom in

While using Markup in a supported app, pinch open so you can draw, adjust shapes, and more, up close. To pan when you're zoomed in, drag two fingers. To zoom back out, pinch closed.

Magnify

In the Markup toolbar in a supported app, tap the Add Annotation button, then tap Magnifier.

Note: If you don't see the Markup toolbar, tap the Markup Switch button off or Markup. If the toolbar is minimized, tap its minimized version.

To change the magnifier's characteristics, do any of the following:

- Change the magnification level: Drag the green dot on the magnifier.

- Change the size of the magnifier: Drag the blue dot on the magnifier.

- Move the magnifier: Drag it.

- Change the outline thickness of the magnifier: Tap the Shapes Attribute button 🖿, then choose an option.

- Change the outline color of the magnifier: Choose an option from the color picker.

- Remove or duplicate the magnifier: Tap its outline, then tap Delete or Duplicate.

To hide the Markup toolbar when you finish, tap the Markup Switch button on or **Done**.

Install and manage app extensions on iPad

Some apps let you extend the functionality of your iPad. An app extension may appear as a sharing option, an action option, a widget in Today View, a file provider, or a custom keyboard.

App extensions can also help you edit a photo or video in your Photos app. For example, you can download a photo-related app to apply filters to photos.

Download and install app extensions

1. Download the app from the App Store.

2. Open the app, then follow the onscreen instructions.

Manage sharing or action options

1. Tap the Share button ⬆️, then tap More. (You may need to swipe the options left to reveal More.)

2. Turn the sharing or action options on or off.

3. To reorder the options, touch and drag the Reorder button ≡.

4. Tap Done.

Open two items in Split View on iPad

Open two different apps, or two windows from the same app, by splitting the screen into resizable views. For example, open Messages and Maps at the same time in Split View. Or open two Messages windows in Split View and manage two conversations at the same time.

Open a second item in Split View

1. While using an app, swipe up from the bottom edge and pause to reveal the Dock.

2. Touch and hold an app in the Dock, drag it to the right or left edge of the screen, then lift your finger.

3. If two items are already open in Split View, drag over the item you want to replace.

4. To give both views equal space, drag the divider to the center of the screen.

Drag to resize the split.

Close Split View

Drag the app divider to the left or right edge of the screen, depending on which app you want to close.

Turn Split View into Slide Over

Swipe down from the top of the smaller view.

Open an app in Slide Over on iPad

You can use an app that slides in front of another app or in front of itself. For example, open Messages in Slide Over to carry on a conversation while using Maps.

iPad keeps track of the apps you open in Slide Over so that you can switch between them easily.

Open another app in Slide Over

1. While using an app, swipe up from the bottom edge and pause to reveal the Dock.

2. Touch and hold an app in the Dock, then drag it above the Dock.

If an app is already open in Slide Over, it's replaced by the app you drag from the Dock.

To open a third app in Slide Over when the screen is in Split View (on supported models), drag the app from the Dock to the Split View divider.

Switch between apps in Slide Over

Swipe right along the bottom of the Slide Over window, or do the following:

1. Swipe up from the bottom of the Slide Over window.

2. Swipe right, then tap the window you want to view.

Move the Slide Over window

- Do one of the following:

- Move the Slide Over window to the other side of the screen: Drag from the top of the Slide Over window.

- Remove the Slide Over window: Drag the top of the window off the right edge of the screen.

Turn Slide Over into Split View

Drag the top of the Slide Over window to the lower right or lower left of the screen.

On supported models, you can use Slide Over and Split View simultaneously.

View all of an app's workspaces

You can view all open windows for an app, including those in Split View and Slide Over.

- From an open app: Tap the app icon in the Dock.

- Swipe up from the bottom edge of the screen if you don't see the Dock.

- From the Home screen: Touch and hold an app icon, then choose the Show All Windows quick action.

  For an app in the Dock, swipe up from the bottom edge of the screen if you don't see the Dock.

Note: If you touch and hold an app icon for too long before choosing a quick action, the icons begin to jiggle. Tap Done or press the Home button (models with a Home button), then try again.

Multitask with Picture in Picture on iPad

With Picture in Picture, you can use FaceTime or watch a video while you use other apps.

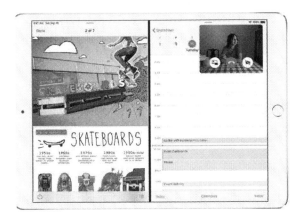

When using FaceTime or watching a video, tap the Picture in Picture Start button or press the Home button (models with the Home button).

The video window scales down to a corner of your display so you can see the Home screen and open other apps. With the video window showing, you can do any of the following:

- Resize the video window: To make the small video window larger, pinch open. To shrink it again, pinch closed.

- Show and hide controls: Tap the video window.

- Move the video window: Drag it to a different corner of the screen.

68

- Hide the video window: Drag it off the left or right edge of the screen.

- Close the video window: Tap the Close button .

- Return to a full FaceTime or video screen: Tap the Picture in Picture button ⌐⌐ in the small video window.

Move items with drag and drop on iPad

With drag and drop, you can use a finger to move text and items within an app and copy items from one app to another. For example, you can drag an image from Notes into an email. (Not all third-party apps support drag and drop.)

Move an item

1. Touch and hold the item until it lifts up (if it's text, select it first).

2. Drag it to another location within the app.

3. If you drag to the bottom or top of a long document, it automatically scrolls.

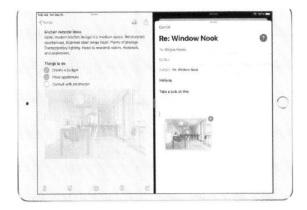

Copy an item between open apps

1. Open two apps in Split View or in Slide Over, then touch and hold the item until it lifts up (if it's text, select it first).

2. Drag it to the other app.

3. As you drag, the Insert icon ⊕ appears wherever you can drop the item. If you drag to the bottom or top of a long document, it automatically scrolls.

Tip: If you want to drag the item to a new note or email, for example, open the new note or email first so you can drag the item directly to it.

Drag a link to a Split View or Slide Over window

Touch and hold the link until it lifts up, then do one of the following:

- Replace a Split View or Slide Over window with the link's destination: Drag the link to the window.

- Open the link's destination in a Split View of Slide Over window: When there is no Split View or Slide Over window showing, drag the link to the left or right edge of the screen to open the destination in Split View, or drag the link close to the edge to open in Slide Over.

Copy an item to an app on the Home screen or in the Dock

1. Touch and hold the item until it lifts up (if it's text, select it first).

2. While you continue to hold the item, use another finger to swipe up from the bottom edge of the screen and pause to reveal the Dock or press the Home button (models with the Home button).

3. Drag the item over the other app to open it (a ghost image of the item appears under your finger as you drag).

You can drag over items in the app to navigate to where you want to drop the item (as you drag, the Insert icon appears wherever you can drop the item). For example, you can drag over the notes list to open the note where you want to drop the item, or you can use another finger to open a new note where you can drop the item.

If you change your mind about moving an item, lift your finger before dragging, or drag the item off the screen.

Select multiple items to move

1. Touch and hold the first selected item, drag it slightly, and continue holding it.

2. While still holding the first item, tap additional items with another finger. A badge indicates the number of selected items.

3. Drag all of the items together.

If you change your mind about moving items, lift your finger before dragging, or drag the items off the screen.

Use AirDrop on iPad to send items to devices near you

With AirDrop you can wirelessly send your photos, videos, websites, locations, and more to other nearby devices and Mac computers (iOS 7, iPadOS 13, OS X 10.10, or later required). AirDrop transfers information using Wi-Fi and Bluetooth—both must be turned on. To use AirDrop, you need to be signed in with your Apple ID. Transfers are encrypted for security.

Send an item using AirDrop

1. Open the item, then tap the Share button, Share, AirDrop, the More options button, or another button that displays the app's sharing options.

2. Do one of the following:

- Tap the AirDrop icon 🌐 in the row of share options, then tap the profile picture of a nearby AirDrop user.

- Above the row of share options, choose one of the people you know who have nearby devices available for AirDrop. Their profile pictures appear with the AirDrop icon.

If the person doesn't appear as a nearby AirDrop user, ask them to open Control Center on iPhone, iPad, or iPod touch and allow AirDrop to receive items. To send to someone on a Mac, ask them to allow themselves to be discovered in AirDrop in the Finder.

To send an item using a method other than AirDrop, choose the method—for example, Messages or Mail—from the row of sharing options (options vary by app). Siri may also suggest ways to share with the people you know by displaying their profile pictures and icons representing sharing methods.

You can also use AirDrop to securely share app and website passwords with someone using an iPhone, iPad, iPod touch, or a Mac.

Allow others to send items to your iPad using AirDrop

1. Open Control Center, then tap the AirDrop icon.

If you don't see the AirDrop icon, touch and hold the top-left group of controls.

2. Tap Contacts Only or Everyone to choose who you want to receive items from.

You can accept or decline each request as it arrives.

Quit and restart an app on iPad

If an app isn't working properly, you can quit it and then try to reopen it. Restarting the app may resolve the problem. (Typically, there is no reason to quit an app; quitting it doesn't save battery power, for example.)

1. To quit an app, open the App Switcher, then swipe up on the app.

2. To restart the app, go to the Home screen, then tap the app.

If restarting the app doesn't solve your problem, try restarting iPad.

Get apps, games, and fonts in the App Store on iPad

In the App Store app , you can discover new apps and games, download custom fonts, and learn tips and tricks. You can also subscribe to Apple Arcade (not available in all countries or regions) and access new games on iPhone, iPad, iPod touch, Mac, and Apple TV.

Find apps, games, and fonts

Ask Siri. Say something like: "Search the App Store for cooking apps" or "Get the Minecraft app."

You can also tap any of the following:

- Today: Discover featured stories and apps.

- Games or Apps: Explore new releases, see the top charts, or browse by category.

- Arcade: Subscribe to Apple Arcade and access new games on your iPhone, iPad, iPod touch, Mac, and Apple TV.

- Search: Enter what you're looking for, then tap Search on the keyboard.

Buy and download an app

1. To buy an app, tap the price. If the app is free, tap Get.

If you see the Download button instead of a price, you already purchased the app, and you can download it again without a charge.

2. If required, authenticate your Apple ID with Face ID, Touch ID, or your passcode to complete your purchase.

While the app is downloading, its icon appears on the Home screen with a progress indicator.

Install fonts

You can get fonts from the App Store to use in documents you create on iPad.

1. After you download an app containing fonts from the App Store, open the app to install the fonts.

2. To manage installed fonts, go to Settings > General > Fonts.

Share or give an app

1. Tap the app to see its details.

2. Tap the More button ***, then tap Share or Gift App (not available for all apps).

Give or redeem an App Store & iTunes gift card

1. Tap the My Account button or your profile picture at the top right.

2. Tap one of the following:

- Redeem Gift Card or Code

- Send Gift Card by Email

Note: You need an Internet connection and an Apple ID to use the App Store. The availability of the App Store and Apple Arcade varies by country or region. Not all Apple Arcade content shown may be available at service availability.

Manage your App Store purchases, subscriptions, and settings on iPad

In the App Store app, you can manage subscriptions and review and download purchases made by you or other family members. You can also customize your preferences for the App Store in Settings.

Approve purchases with Family Sharing

With Family Sharing set up, the family organizer can review and approve purchases made by other family members under a certain age.

View and redownload eligible apps purchased by you or family members

1. Tap the My Account button ⊚ or your profile picture at the top right, then tap Purchased.

2. If you set up Family Sharing, tap My Purchases or choose a family member to view their purchases.

Note: You can see purchases made by family members only if they choose to share their purchases. Purchases made with Family Sharing may not be accessible after the family member leaves the family group.

3. Find the app you want to download, then tap the Download button ⌂.

Manage your subscriptions

Tap the My Account button ⊚ or your profile picture at the top right, then tap Subscriptions.

Change your App Store settings

Go to Settings > [your name] > iTunes & App Store, then do any of the following:

- Automatically download apps purchased on your other Apple devices: Below Automatic Downloads, turn on Apps.

- Automatically update apps: Turn on App Updates.

- Control the use of cellular data for app downloads: (Wi-Fi + Cellular models) To allow downloads to use cellular data, turn on Automatic Downloads. To choose whether you want to be asked for permission for downloads over 200 MB or all apps, tap App Downloads.

- Automatically play app preview videos: Turn on Video Autoplay.

Find and buy books from Apple Books on iPad

With the Books app , you can purchase books and audiobooks directly from Apple Books and then read or listen to them right in the app.

1. Open Books, then tap Book Store or Audiobooks to browse titles, or tap Search to look for a specific title.

2. Tap a book cover to see more details, read or listen to a sample, or add the book to your Want to Read collection.

3. Tap Buy to purchase a title, or tap Get to download a free title.

All purchases are made with the payment method associated with your Apple ID.

Read books in the Books app on iPad

In the Books app , use the Reading Now and Library tabs at the bottom of the screen to see the books you're currently reading, get personalized recommendations, learn about new releases, and keep track of the books you want to read.

Reading Now: Tap to access the last book or audiobook that you were reading. You can also see items that you added to your Want To Read list and recommendations based on the books you've purchased.

Library: Tap to see all of the books, audiobooks, series, and PDFs that you got from the Book Store or manually added to your library.

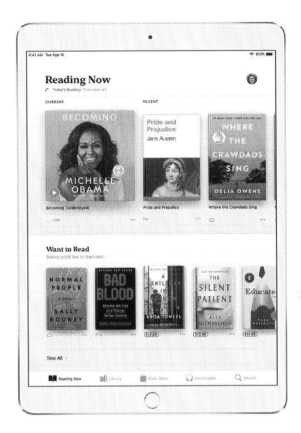

Read a book

Tap the Reading Now or Library tab, then tap a cover to open a book. Use gestures and controls to navigate as follows:

1. Turn the page: Tap the right side of the page or swipe right to left.

2. Go back to the previous page: Tap the left side of the page or swipe left to right.

3. Go to a specific page: Tap the page and move the slider at the bottom of the screen left or right. Or, tap the Search button and enter a page number, then tap the page number in the search results.

4. Close a book: Tap the center of the page to show the controls, then tap the Back button.

Tip: Turn iPad to landscape orientation to view two pages at once.

Change text and display appearance

Tap the page, tap the Appearance button, then do any of the following:

- Adjust the screen brightness: Drag the slider left or right.

- Change the font size: Tap the large A to increase the font size or tap the small A to decrease it.

- Change the font: Tap Fonts to choose a different font.

- Change the page background color: Tap a colored circle.

- Dim the screen when it's dark: Turn on Auto-Night Theme to automatically change the page color and brightness when using Books in low-light conditions. (Not all books support Auto-Night Theme.)

- Turn off pagination: Turn Scrolling View on to scroll continuously through the book.

Bookmark a page

When you close a book, your place is saved automatically—you don't need to add a bookmark. Bookmark pages you want to return to again. Tap the Bookmark Ribbon ⎙ to add a bookmark; tap it again to remove the Bookmark.

To see all your bookmarks, tap the Table of Contents button ▤, then tap Bookmarks.

Highlight or underline text

1. Touch and hold a word, then move the grab points to adjust the selection.

2. Tap Highlight, then tap Highlight Color Chooser
   ◑ to choose a highlight color or underline.

   To remove a highlight or underline, tap the text,
   then tap the Trash button 🗑.

To see all of your highlights, tap the Table of Contents
button, then tap Notes.

Add a note

1. Touch and hold a word, then move the grab
   points to adjust the selection.

2. Tap Note, then enter note text.

3. Tap the page to close the note and continue
   reading.

To see all of your notes, tap the Table of Contents
button, then tap Notes. Swipe left on a note to delete
it.

Share a selection

You can send text selections using AirDrop, Mail, or
Messages, or you can add the selection to Notes. If the
book is from the Book Store, a link to the book is

included with the selection. (Sharing may not be available in all regions.)

1. Touch and hold a word, then move the grab points to adjust the selection.

2. Tap Share, then choose a method.

You can also send a link to view the book in the Book Store. Tap a page, tap the Table of Contents button, then tap the Share button 📤.

Access your books on all your devices

You can keep your Books information updated across your iPhone, iPad, and iPod touch where you're signed in to iCloud with the same Apple ID.

• Reading Now and Library: Go to Settings > [your name] > iCloud, and turn on both iCloud Drive and Books. Then go to Settings > Books, and turn on Reading Now.

• Reading position, notes, and highlights: Go to Settings > [your name] > iCloud, then turn on both iCloud Drive and Books.

On your Mac, choose Apple menu > System Preferences, then do one of the following:

- macOS Catalina: Click Apple ID, select iCloud in the sidebar, then select iCloud Drive. Click Options, then select Books.

- macOS 10.14 or earlier: Select iCloud, then select iCloud Drive. Click Options, then select Books.

Listen to audiobooks in Books on iPad

Use the Books app to listen to audiobooks on your iPad.

The audiobook player screen showing the audiobook cover in the center. Above the cover are the track number, audiobook name, and author. Below the cover are the playhead, play, pause, and skip back and skip forward controls. At the bottom of the screen, from left to right, are the Playback Speed button, Sleep Timer button, Playback Destination button, and Share button. The Track List button is at the top right and the Close button is at the top left.

Play an audiobook

In Reading Now or in the Audiobooks collection in your Library, tap the cover, then do any of the following:

- Skip forward or back: Touch and hold the rounded arrows, or slide and hold the book cover. To change the number of seconds that skipping advances, go to Settings > Books.

- Speed it up, or slow it down: Tap the playback speed in the lower-left corner to choose a different speed. 1x is normal speed, 0.75x is three-quarters speed, and so on.

- Set a sleep timer: Tap the Sleep button ☾, then choose a duration.

- Go to a chapter: Tap the Table of Contents button, then tap a chapter.

Note: Some audiobooks refer to chapters as tracks, or don't define chapters.

- Go to a specific time: Drag the playhead, directly below the audiobook cover. The point where you started listening is marked with a gray circle on the timeline. Tap the circle to jump back to that spot.

Set Reading Goals in Books on iPad

The Books app helps you keep track of how many minutes you read every day, and how many books and audiobooks you finish each year. You can customize your goals to spend more time reading, set new reading streaks, and share your achievements with friends.

Change your daily reading goal

You can adjust your daily reading goal depending on how many minutes you want to read per day. If you don't customize your daily reading goal, it's set to five minutes per day.

1. Tap the Reading Now tab, then swipe down to Reading Goals.

2. Tap Today's Reading, then tap Adjust Goal.

3. Slide the counter up or down to set the minutes per day that you want to read.

When you reach your daily reading goal, you receive a notification from Books; tap it to get more details about your achievement, or send your achievement to friends.

Note: To count PDFs toward your reading goal, go to Settings > Books > then turn on Include PDFs.

Change your yearly reading goal

After you finish reading a book or audiobook in Books, the Books Read This Year collection appears below Reading Goals. The default yearly reading goal is three books per year, but you can increase or decrease your goal depending on how many books you want to finish.

1. Tap the Reading Now tab, then swipe down to Books Read This Year.

2. Tap a gray placeholder square, or a book cover, then tap Adjust Goal.

3. Slide the counter up or down to set the books per year that you want to read.

When you reach your yearly reading goal, you receive a notification from Books; tap it to get more details about your achievement, or send your achievement to friends.

See your reading streaks and records

Books lets you know how many days in a row you reach your daily reading goal and notifies you when you set a record.

To view your current reading streak and record, tap the Reading Now tab, then swipe down to Reading Goals.

Turn off notifications and Reading Goals

Turn off notifications: To stop receiving notifications when you achieve a reading goal or set a reading streak, tap your account in the top-right corner of the

Reading Now tab, tap Notifications, then turn off Reading Goals.

Turn off Reading Goals: Go to Settings > Books > then turn off Reading Goals. When Reading Goals is turned off, the reading indicators in Reading Now are hidden and you don't receive notifications.

Organize books in the Books app on iPad

In the Books app , the books and audiobooks you purchase are saved in your library and automatically sorted into collections, such as Audiobooks, Want to Read, and Finished.

Create a collection and add books to it

You can create your own collections to personalize your library.

1. Tap Library, tap Collections, then tap New Collection.

2. Name the collection, for example, Beach Reads or Book Club, then tap Done.

3. To add a book to the collection, tap the More Info button ••• below the book cover (or on the

book's details page in the Book Store), tap Add
to Collection, then choose the collection.

You can add the same book to multiple collections.

Sort books in your library

Tap Library, tap Sort, then choose Recent, Title,
Author, or Manually.

Tap the Table of Contents button to view books by title
or cover.

Remove books, audiobooks, and PDFs

You can remove books, audiobooks, and PDFs from
Reading Now and your library collections, or hide them
on your iPad.

1. Tap Library, then tap Edit.

For audiobooks, tap Library, then go to the Audiobooks
collection.

1. Tap the items you want to remove.

2. Tap the Trash button and select an option.

To unhide books that you have hidden, tap Reading
Now, tap your account icon, then tap Manage Hidden
Purchases.

Access your library across devices

You can sync your Library and collections across all your devices where you are signed in with the same Apple ID. Go to Settings > [your name] > iCloud, turn on iCloud Drive, then turn on Books.

Read PDF documents in Books on iPad

In the Books app, you can open and save PDFs that you receive in Mail, Messages, and other apps.

Open PDFs in Books

Do one of the following:

- Touch and hold the PDF attachment, then tap Copy to Books.

- Tap the PDF attachment to open it, tap the Share button ⬆️, then tap Copy to Books.

Email or print a PDF document

Open the PDF document, tap the Share button, then choose Mail or Print.

Mark up a PDF

Open the PDF and tap the Markup button to use the drawing and annotation tools (tap near the center of a page if you don't see the Markup button Ⓐ).

View PDFs across devices

You can see PDFs and books that are not from the BookStore across your iPhone, iPad, iPod touch, and Mac where you're signed in with the same Apple ID.

Go to Settings > [your name] > iCloud, turn on iCloud Drive, then turn on Books. Then go to Settings > Books, and turn on iCloud Drive.

Create and edit events in Calendar on iPad

Use the Calendar app 🔟 to create and edit events, appointments, and meetings.

View invitations.

Change calendars
or accounts.

Ask Siri. Say something like:

"Set up a meeting with Gordon at 9"

"Do I have a meeting at 10?"

"Where is my 3:30 meeting?"

Add an event

1. In day view, tap the Add button + at the top
   right.

2. Fill in the event details.

Enter the name and location of the event, the start and end times, how often it repeats, and so on.

3. Tap Add at the top right.

Add an alert

You can set an alert to be reminded of an event beforehand.

1. Tap the event, then tap Edit at the top right.

2. In the event details, tap Alert.

3. Choose when you want to be reminded.

For example, "At time of event," "5 minutes before," or another choice.

Note: If you add the address of the event's location, Calendar uses Apple Maps to look up locations, traffic conditions, and transit options to tell you when it's time to leave.

Add an attachment

You can add an attachment to a Calendar event to share with invitees.

1. Tap the event, then tap Edit at the top right.

2. In the event details, tap Add attachment.

The Files app opens, displaying your recently opened files.

3. Locate the file you want to attach.

To find the file, you can scroll, tap folders to open them, tap Browse to look in other locations (such as iCloud Drive), enter a file name in the search field, and so on.

4. **Tap Done.**

To remove the attachment, tap the event, tap Edit at the top right, swipe left over the attachment, then tap Remove.

Find events in other apps

Siri can suggest events found in Mail, Messages, and Safari—such as flight reservations and hotel bookings—so you can add them easily in Calendar.

1. Go to Settings > Calendar > Siri & Search.

2. Turn on Show Siri Suggestions in App to allow Siri to suggest events found in other apps.

To allow Siri to make suggestions in other apps based on how you use Calendar, turn on Learn from this App.

View events sent to you in Mail or other apps

1. Go to Settings > Calendar > Siri & Search.

2. Turn on Find Events in Other Apps.

Edit an event

You can change the time of an event and any of the other event details.

1. Change the time: In day view, touch and hold the event, then drag it to a new time, or adjust the grab points.

2. Change event details: Tap the event, tap Edit at the top right, then in the event details, tap a setting to change it, or tap in a field to type in new information.

Delete an event

In day view, tap the event, then tap Delete Event at the bottom of the screen.

Send and receive invitations in Calendar on iPad

In the Calendar app, send and receive meeting and event invitations. iCloud, Microsoft Exchange, and some CalDAV servers let you send and receive meeting invitations. (Not all calendar servers support every feature.)

Invite others to an event

You can invite people to an event, even if you're not the one who scheduled it, with Exchange and other servers.

1. Tap the event, tap Edit, tap Invitees, then tap Add Invitees.

   Or, if you didn't schedule the event, tap it, tap Invitees, then tap the Send Mail to Invitees button ✉

2. Type the names or email addresses of invitees, or tap the Add button to browse your Contacts.

3. Tap Done (or tap Send if you didn't schedule the event).

With Microsoft Exchange, and some other servers, you can invite people to an event even if you're not the one who scheduled it.

If you don't want to be notified when someone declines a meeting, go to Settings > Calendar, then turn off Show Invitee Declines.

Reply to an event invitation

1. To respond to an event notification, tap it.

   Or, in Calendar, tap Inbox, then tap an invitation.

2. Tap your response—Accept, Maybe, or Decline.

To respond to an invitation you receive by email, tap the underlined text in the email, then tap Show in Calendar.

If you add comments to your response (comments may not be available for all calendars), your comments can be seen by the organizer but not by other attendees. To see events you declined, tap Calendars at the bottom of the screen, then turn on Show Declined Events.

Schedule a meeting without blocking your schedule

You can add an event to your calendar without having the time frame appear as busy to others who send you invitations.

1. Tap the event, then tap Edit.

2. Tap Show As, then tap Free.

Suggest a different meeting time

You can suggest a different time for a meeting invitation you've received.

1. Tap the meeting, then tap Propose New Time.

2. Tap the time, then enter a new one.

3. Tap Done, then tap Send.

Quickly send an email to attendees

Tap an event that has attendees.

Tap Invitees, then tap the Send Mail to Invitees button.

Change how you view events in Calendar on iPad

In the Calendar app, you can view one day, a week, a month, or a year at a time, or view a list of upcoming events. To change your view of Calendar, do any of the following:

- Zoom in or out: Tap Day, Week, Month, Year at the top of the screen to zoom in or out on your calendar. In week or day view, pinch to zoom in or out.

- View upcoming events: Tap the Search button Q to view upcoming events as a list.

Search for events in Calendar on iPad

In the Calendar app, you can search for events by title, invitees, location, and notes.

Tap the Search button, then enter the text you want to find in the search field. Ask Siri. Say something like: "What's on my calendar for Friday?"

Customize your calendar on iPad

In the Calendar app, you can choose which day of the week Calendar starts with, display week numbers, choose alternate calendars (for example, to display

Chinese or Hebrew dates), override the automatic time zone, and more.

Go to Settings > Calendar, then choose the settings and features you want.

Keep track of events in Calendar on iPad

In the Calendar app, you can customize the notifications that let you know about upcoming Calendar events, invitations, and more. You can also make sure your events and other calendar information are kept up to date on all your devices.

Customize Calendar notifications

1. Go to Settings > Notifications > Calendar.

2. Turn on Allow Notifications.

3. Tap a type of event (for example, Upcoming Events), then choose how and where you want the notifications for those events to appear—for example, on the Lock screen, in Notification Center, as banners at the top of the screen, with an alert sound, and so on.

Keep your Calendar up to date across your devices

You can use iCloud to keep your Calendar information up to date on all your devices where you're signed in with the same Apple ID.

Go to Settings > [your name] > iCloud, then turn on Calendar.

If you don't want to use iCloud for your Calendar, you can sync your Calendar information between your iPad and your computer.

Set up multiple calendars on iPad

In the Calendar app , set up multiple calendars to keep track of different kinds of events. Although you can keep track of all your events and appointments in one place, you don't have to. Additional calendars are easy to set up, and a great way to stay organized.

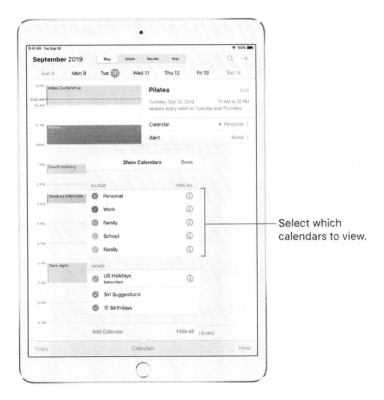

Select which calendars to view.

See multiple calendars at once

To view multiple calendars, tap Calendars at the bottom of the screen, then do any of the following:

- Select the calendars you want to view.

- Tap US Holidays to include national holidays with your events.

- Tap Birthdays to include birthdays from Contacts with your events.

Set a default calendar

You can set one of your calendars as the default calendar. When you add an event using Siri or other apps, it's added to your default calendar.

1. Go to Settings > Calendar > Default Calendar.

2. Select the calendar you want to use as your default calendar.

Change a calendar's color

1. Tap Calendars at the bottom of the screen.

2. Tap the Info button next to the calendar, then choose a color.

3. Tap Done.

For some calendar accounts, such as Google, the color is set by the server.

Turn on iCloud, Google, Exchange, or Yahoo calendars

1. Go to Settings > Passwords & Accounts > Add Account > Other.

2. Tap Add CalDAV Account or Add Subscribed Calendar.

3. Enter the server information.

Subscribe to a calendar

1. Go to Settings > Passwords & Accounts > Add Account > Other.

2. Tap Add Subscribed Calendar.

3. Enter the URL of the .the statistics file to subscribe to and any other required server information.

You can also subscribe to an iCalendar (. statistics) calendar by tapping a link to the calendar.

Add a CalDAV account

1. Go to Settings > Passwords & Accounts > Add Account > Other.

2. Tap Add CalDAV account.

3. Enter the server information.

Move an event to another calendar

Tap the event, tap Calendar, then select a calendar to move the event to.

Set reminders on iPad

In the Reminders app , you can easily create and organize reminders to keep track of all of life's to-dos. Use it for shopping lists, projects at work, tasks around the house, and anything else you want to track. Create subtasks, set flags, add attachments, and choose when and where to receive reminders. You can also use smart lists to automatically organize your reminders.

A Reminders screen showing reminder lists on the left side, and a list called Camping Trip on the right side. Tap a reminder to mark it as completed.

Keep your reminders up to date on all your devices with iCloud

Go to Settings > [your name] > iCloud, then turn on Reminders.

Your iCloud reminders—and any changes you make to them—appear on your iPhone, iPad, iPod touch, Apple Watch, and Mac where you're signed in with your Apple ID.

Note: If you've been using an earlier version of Reminders, you may need to upgrade your iCloud reminders to use features such as attachments, flags, subtasks, grouped lists, list colors and icons, and more. To upgrade, tap the Upgrade button next to your iCloud account in Reminders. (You may need to tap Lists at the top left to see your iCloud account.)

Also note the following:

- Upgraded reminders are not backward compatible with the Reminders app in earlier versions of iOS and macOS.

- Until macOS Catalina is available, your Mac using the same iCloud account can't access your upgraded reminders.

Add a reminder

Ask Siri. Say something like: "Add artichokes to my groceries list." Or do the following in a list:

- Tap New Reminder, then enter text.

- Use the quick toolbar above the keyboard to do any of the following:

- Schedule a date or time: Tap the Time button, then choose a date for an all-day reminder or tap Custom to set a date and time for the notification.

- Add a location: Tap the Location button, then choose where you want to be reminded—for example, when you leave work or arrive at home.

- Set a flag: Tap the Flag button to mark an important reminder.

- Attach a photo or scanned document: Tap the Photos button, then take a new photo, choose an existing photo from your photo library, or scan a document.

- To add more details to the reminder, tap the Edit Details button, then do any of the following:

- Add notes: In the Notes field, enter more info about the reminder.

- Add a web link: In the URL field, enter a web address. Reminders displays the link as a thumbnail that you can tap to go to the website.

- Get a reminder when chatting with someone in Messages: Turn on "Remind me when messaging," then choose someone from your contacts list. The reminder appears the next time you chat with that person in Messages.

- Set a priority: Tap Priority, then choose an option.

- Tap Done.

Completed reminders are hidden the next time you view the list. To unhide completed reminders, tap the More button, then tap Show Completed.

Move or delete reminders

- Reorder reminders in a list: Touch and hold a reminder you want to move, then drag it to a new location.

- Make a subtask: Swipe right on the reminder, then tap Indent. Or drag a reminder onto another reminder.

- If you delete or move a parent task, the subtasks are also deleted or moved. If you complete a parent task, the subtasks are also completed.

- Move a reminder to a different list: Tap the reminder, tap the Edit Details button, tap List, then choose a list.

- Delete a reminder: Swipe left on the reminder, then tap Delete.

- To recover a deleted reminder, shake to undo or swipe left with three fingers.

Change your Reminders settings

- Go to Settings > Reminders.

- Choose options such as the following:

- Default List: Choose the list for new reminders you create outside of a specific list, such as reminders you create using Siri.

- Today Notification: Set a time to show notifications in Today View for all-day reminders that have been assigned a date without a time.

- Show Reminders as Overdue: The scheduled date turns red for overdue all-day reminders.

Chapter 4
Siri

How to Ask Siri on iPad

Talking to Siri is a quick way to get things done. Ask Siri to translate a phrase, set a timer, find a location, report on the weather, and more. The more you use Siri, the better it knows what you need.

To use Siri, iPad must be connected to the Internet. Cellular charges may apply.

Set up Siri

If you didn't set up Siri when you first set up your iPad, go to Settings > Siri & Search, then turn on the following:

- Listen for "Hey Siri"

- Press Home for Siri (models with the Home button) or Press Top Button for Siri (other models)

Summon Siri with your voice

- Say "Hey Siri," then ask Siri a question or to do a task for you.

- For example, say something like "Hey Siri, how's the weather today?" or "Hey Siri, set an alarm for 8 a.m."

- To ask Siri another question or to do another task, tap the Listen button.

Note: To prevent iPad from responding to "Hey Siri," place your iPad face down, or go to Settings > Siri & Search, then turn off Listen for "Hey Siri."

Summon Siri with a button

Do one of the following:

- Models with the Home button: Press and hold the Home button.

- Other models: Press and hold the top button.

- When Siri appears, ask Siri a question or to do a task for you.

- For example, say something like "What's 18 percent of 225?" or "Set the timer for 3 minutes."

- To ask Siri another question or to do another task, tap the Listen button.

Make a correction if Siri misunderstands you

- Rephrase your request: Tap the Listen button, then say your request in a different way.

- Spell out part of your request: Tap the Listen button, then repeat your request by spelling out any words that Siri didn't understand. For example, say "Call," then spell the person's name.

- Edit your request with text: Above the response from Siri, tap "Tap to Edit," then use the onscreen keyboard.

- Change a message before sending it: Say "Change it."

Type instead of speaking to Siri

- Go to Settings > Accessibility > Siri, then turn on Type to Siri.

- To make a request, summon Siri, then use the keyboard and text field to ask Siri a question or to do a task for you.

Siri is designed to protect your information, and you can choose what you share. To learn more, go to Settings > Siri & Search > About Ask Siri & Privacy.

Find out what Siri can do on iPad

Use Siri on iPad to get information and perform tasks.

- **Find answers to your questions:** Find information from the web, get sports scores, get arithmetic calculations, and more. Say something like "Hey Siri, what causes a rainbow," "Hey Siri, what was the score of the Orioles game yesterday," or "Hey Siri, what's the derivative of cosine x?"

When Siri displays a web link, you can tap it to see more information in Safari.

- **Perform tasks with apps on iPad**: Use Siri to control apps with your voice. For example, to create an event in Calendar, say something like "Hey Siri, set up a meeting with Gordon at 9," or to add an item to Reminders, say something like "Hey Siri, add artichokes to my groceries list."

When the onscreen response from Siri includes buttons or controls, you can tap them to take further action.

- **Translate languages**: Say something like "Hey Siri, how do you say Thank You in Mandarin?" or "Hey Siri, what languages can you translate?"

In response to the question "How do you say thank you in Mandarin?," Siri displays a translation of the English phrase "thank you" into Mandarin. A button to the right of the translation replays audio of the translation.

- **Play a radio station**: Say something like "Hey Siri, play Wild 94.9" or "Hey Siri, tune into ESPN Radio."

- Let Siri show you more examples: Say something like "Hey Siri, what can you do?" You can also tap the Help button after you summon Siri.

About Siri Suggestions on iPad

Siri makes suggestions for what you might want to do next, such as confirm an appointment or send an email, based on your routines and how you use your apps. For example, Siri might help when you do any of the following:

- **Glance at the Lock screen or start a search**: As Siri learns your routines, you get suggestions for just what you need, at just the right time. For example, if you frequently order coffee mid morning, Siri may suggest your order near the time you normally place it.

- **Create email and events**: When you start adding people to an email or calendar event, Siri suggests the people you included in previous emails or events.

- **Leave for an event**: If your calendar event includes a location, Siri assesses traffic conditions and notifies you when to leave.

- **See your flight status**: If you have a boarding pass in Mail, Siri shows your flight status in Maps. You can tap the suggestion when you're ready to get directions to the airport.

- **Type**: As you enter text, Siri can suggest names of movies, places—anything you viewed on iPad recently. If you tell a friend you're on your way, Siri can even suggest your estimated arrival time.

- **Search in Safari**: Siri suggests websites and other information in the search field as you type.

- (iPad Air 2 and later) Above the keyboard, Siri also suggests words and phrases based on what you were just reading.

- **Confirm an appointment or book a flight on a travel website:** (iPad Air 2 and later) Siri asks if you want to add it to your calendar.

123

- **Read News stories**: As Siri learns which topics you're interested in, they'll be suggested in News.

To turn off Siri Suggestions, go to Settings > Siri & Search, then turn off any of the following:

- Suggestions in Search

- Suggestions in Lookup

- Suggestions on Lock Screen

For a specific app, tap the app, then turn off Show Siri Suggestions.

Your personal information—which is encrypted and remains private—stays up to date across all your devices where you're signed in with the same Apple ID. As Siri learns about you on one device, your experience with Siri is improved on your other devices.

Siri is designed to protect your information, and you can choose what you share. To learn more, go to Settings   > Siri & Search > About Search Suggestions & Privacy.

Change Siri settings on iPad

You can change the voice for Siri, prevent access to Siri when your device is locked, and more. Go to Settings > Siri & Search, then do any of the following:

- **Change the voice for Siri**: (not available in all languages) Tap Siri Voice, then choose a male or female voice for Siri or change the accent.

- Prevent Siri from responding to the voice command "Hey Siri": Turn off Listen for "Hey Siri."

- Prevent Siri from responding to the Home button or the top button: Turn off Press Home for Siri (models with the Home button) or Press Top Button for Siri (other models).

- Change the language Siri responds to: Tap Language.

- Limit when Siri provides voice feedback: If you don't want Siri to always provide voice feedback, tap Voice Feedback, then choose an option.

125

- Prevent access to Siri when iPad is locked: Turn off Allow Siri When Locked.

Adjust the Siri voice volume

Ask Siri. Say something like: "Turn up the volume" or "Turn down the volume."

Chapter 5
Apple Pay

Set up Apple Pay

Set up Apple Pay to make secure payments in apps and on websites that support Apple Pay. In Messages, you can send and receive money from friends and family or make purchases using Business Chat.

Add a credit or debit card

- Go to Settings > Wallet & Apple Pay.
- Tap Add Cards. You may be asked to sign in with your Apple ID.

Do one of the following:

- **Add a new card**: Position iPad so that your card appears in the frame, or enter the card details manually.

- **Add your previous cards**: Select the card associated with your Apple ID, cards you use with Apple Pay on your other devices, or cards that you removed. Tap Continue, then enter the CVV number of each card.

Alternatively, you may be able to add your card from the app of the bank or card issuer.

The card issuer determines whether your card is eligible for Apple Pay, and may ask you for additional information to complete the verification process.

View the information for a card and change its settings

- Go to Settings > Wallet & Apple Pay.
- Tap a card, then do any of the following:
- Tap Transactions to view your recent history. To hide this information, turn off Transaction History. To view all your Apple Pay activity, see the statement from your card issuer.
- View the last four digits of the card number and Device Account Number—the number transmitted to the merchant.
- Change the billing address.
- Remove the card from Apple Pay.

Change your Apple Pay settings

- Go to Settings > Wallet & Apple Pay.
- Do any of the following:

- Set your default card.

- Add the shipping address and contact information for purchases.

Remove your cards from Apple Pay if your iPad is lost or stolen

If you enabled Find My iPhone, use it to help locate and secure your iPad. Do any of the following:

- On a Mac or PC: Sign in to your Apple ID account. In the Devices section, click the lost iPad. Below the list of cards, click Remove all.

- On another iPhone, iPad, or iPod touch: Go to Settings > [your name], tap the lost iPad, then tap Remove All Cards (below Apple Pay).

- Call the issuers of your cards.

If you remove cards, you can add them again later. If you sign out of iCloud in Settings > [your name], all your credit and debit cards for Apple Pay are removed from iPad. You can add the cards again the next time you sign in.

Pay in apps or on the web using Apple Pay on iPad

Use Apple Pay to make purchases in apps and on the web in Safari wherever you see the Apple Pay button.

Pay in an app or on the web

- During checkout, tap the Apple Pay button.
- Review the payment information.
- You can change the credit card, shipping address, and contact information.
- Complete the payment:
- Models with Face ID: Double-click the top button, then glance at iPad to authenticate with Face ID, or enter your passcode.
- Models with Touch ID: Authenticate with Touch ID or enter your passcode.

Change your default shipping and contact information

- Go to Settings > Wallet & Apple Pay.
- Set any of the following:
- Shipping address
- Email
- Phone

Set up and use Apple Cash on iPad (U.S. only)

When you receive money in Messages, it's added to your Apple Cash. You can use Apple Cash right away wherever you would use Apple Pay. You can also transfer your Apple Cash balance to your bank account.

Set up Apple Cash

Do any of the following:

- Go to Settings > Wallet & Apple Pay, then turn on Apple Cash.

- In Messages, send or accept a payment. See Pay in apps or on the web using Apple Pay.

Use Apple Cash

You can use Apple Cash wherever you use Apple Pay:

- Send and receive money with Apple Pay (U.S. only)
- Pay in apps or on the web using Apple Pay
- Manage your Apple Cash

Go to Settings > Wallet & Apple Pay, then tap Apple Cash. Do any of the following:

- Add money from a debit card.
- Transfer money to your bank.
- Update your bank account information.
- Tap Transactions to view your history and details (including comments sent with payments), manually accept or reject individual payments, and request a statement.
- Choose to manually or automatically accept all payments. You have 7 days to manually accept a payment before it's returned to the sender.
- Verify   your   identity   for   account servicing and to increase your transaction limits.
- Contact Apple Support.

Transfer money from Apple Cash to your Visa debit card or bank account

You can transfer money from your Apple Cash1 balance instantly or within 1 to 3 business days.

You can use Instant Transfer to transfer money from your Apple Cash balance to an eligible Visa debit card, or you can use a bank transfer to transfer money to your bank account.

To use Instant Transfer, your iPhone needs to have iOS 12.2 or later. If you are transferring money to a debit card with Instant Transfer, it must be an eligible Visa debit card.

Use Instant Transfer

With Instant Transfer, you can quickly transfer money to an eligible Visa debit card in Wallet. An Instant Transfer is typically available within 30 minutes. Go to your card info:

- **iPhone**: open the Wallet app, tap your Apple Cash card, then tap the more button.
- **iPad**: open the Settings app, tap Wallet & Apple Pay, then tap your Apple Cash card.

- Tap Transfer to Bank.

- Enter an amount and tap Next.

- Tap Instant Transfer.

- If you haven't added a Visa debit card, tap Add Card and follow the instructions on your screen to add one.

- Tap > select the Visa debit card you want to transfer funds to and select the billing information for your chosen debit card.

- Your funds should transfer within 30 minutes.

Transfer in 1 to 3 business days

You can also use a bank transfer to transfer money to your bank account within 1 to 3 business days.

- Go to your card info:

- iPhone: Open the Wallet app, tap your Apple Cash card, then tap the more button.

- iPad: Open the Settings app, tap Wallet & Apple Pay, then tap your Apple Cash card.

- Apple Watch: Transfer money using your iPhone.

- Tap Transfer to Bank.

- Enter an amount and tap Next.

- Choose 1-3 Business Days. If you don't have a bank account set up, follow the instructions on your screen to add one.
- Confirm with Face ID, Touch ID, or passcode.

- Wait for the money to transfer. This can take 1 to 3 business days.

How long does a bank transfer take

If you use Instant Transfer, your funds are typically available in your bank account within 30 minutes.

Bank transfers usually take 1 to 3 business days to complete. Check your bank statement to see if the transfer has been processed and deposited into your bank account. Bank transfers aren't deposited on bank holidays or weekends. See holidays observed by the Federal Reserve on federalreserve.gov.

How to update your bank account information

- Go to your card info:
- iPhone: Open the Wallet app, tap your Apple Cash card, then tap the more button.

- iPad: Open the Settings app, tap Wallet & Apple Pay, then tap your Apple Cash card.
- Apple Watch: Edit the information using your iPhone.
- Tap Bank Account, then tap the bank account you want to update.
- To delete your banking information, tap Delete Bank Account Information. Tap again to confirm. After deleting, you can add your bank information again or add different information.
- To edit your bank information, tap next to your routing number or account number, add your information, then confirm the numbers and tap Next.

After you update your information on one device, it automatically updates on all the devices where you're signed in with your Apple ID.

Chapter 6

Family Sharing

Set up Family Sharing on iPad

With Family Sharing, up to six family members can share iTunes Store, App Store, and Apple Books purchases; an Apple Music family membership; an Apple News+ subscription; an Apple Arcade subscription; an iCloud storage plan; Screen Time information; a family calendar; family photos; and more, all without sharing accounts.

To use Family Sharing, one adult family member (the *organizer*) chooses features for the family to share and invites up to five additional family members to participate. When family members join, Family Sharing is set up on their devices automatically.

Family Sharing requires you (the organizer) to sign in with your Apple ID and to confirm the Apple ID you use for the iTunes Store, the App Store, and Apple Books (you usually use the same Apple ID for everything). Family Sharing is available on devices that meet these minimum system requirements: iOS 8, iPadOS 13, a Mac with OS X 10.10, or a PC with iCloud for Windows 7. You can be part of only one family group at a time.

Note: You can set up Screen Time for individual family members either through Family Sharing on your device or separately on their own devices.

Get started with Family Sharing:

1. Go to Settings ⚙ > [*your name*] > Set Up Family Sharing, then follow the onscreen instructions.

2. Tap the features you want to share:

   - Purchase Sharing

   - iCloud Storage

   - Location Sharing

   - Screen Time

   - Apple Music

   - TV Channels

   - Apple Arcade

- Apple News+

Follow the onscreen instructions to sign up.

Depending on the features you choose, you may be asked to set up an Apple Music family membership or an iCloud Storage subscription. If you choose to share iTunes Store, App Store, and Apple Books purchases with your family members, you agree to pay for any purchases they initiate while part of the family group.

Create an Apple ID for a child

1. Go to Settings ⚙ > [*your name*] > Family Sharing > Add Family Member.

2. Tap Create a Child Account, then follow the onscreen instructions.

The child's account is added to your family until the child is at least 13 years old.

Accept an invitation to Family Sharing

- Tap Accept in the invitation.

Or, if you're near the organizer during the setup process, you can enter your Apple ID and password on the Family Member's Apple ID screen on the organizer's device.

Leave Family Sharing

Any family member can leave the Family Sharing group, but only the organizer can stop family sharing.

1. Go to Settings ⚙ > [*your name*] > Family Sharing > [*your name*].

2. Tap Leave Family.

   If you're the organizer, tap Stop Family Sharing.

Share purchases with family members on iPad

With Family Sharing, up to six family members can share iTunes Store, App Store, and Apple Books purchases, an Apple Music family membership, and an iCloud storage plan.

When your family shares iTunes Store, App Store, and Apple Books purchases, all items are billed directly to the family organizer's Apple ID account. Once purchased, an item is added to the initiating family member's account and eligible purchases are shared with the rest of the family.

Access shared purchases from the iTunes Store

1. Open the iTunes Store ⭐, then tap Purchased.

2. Tap My Purchases at the top left.

3. Choose a family member.

4. Tap a category (for example, Music or Movies) at the top of the screen, tap a purchased item, then tap ⬇ to download it.

Access shared purchases from the App Store

1. Open the App Store 🅰.

2. Tap ⓐ—or your profile picture—at the top right.

3. Tap Purchased, choose a family member, then tap ⬇ next to a purchased item to download it.

Access shared purchases from Apple Books

1. Open the Books app 📖.

2. Tap ⓐ, or your profile picture, at the top right.

3. Tap an item under My Purchases or choose a family member, then tap a category (for example, Books or Audiobooks).

4. Tap All Books, Recent Purchases, or a genre, then tap ⬇ next to a purchased item to download it.

Use a shared iCloud storage plan

With Family Sharing, your family can share an iCloud storage plan of 200 GB or 2 TB.

1. Go to Settings ⚙ > [*your name*] > Family Sharing.

2. Tap iCloud Storage, then follow the onscreen instructions.

You can also purchase or use your own storage plan if you need more space. To upgrade your iCloud storage.

Turn on Ask To Buy on iPad

When your Family Sharing group shares purchases, you can, as the family organizer, require that young family members request approval for purchases or free downloads.

1. Go to Settings ⚙ > [*your name*] > Family Sharing.

2. Tap the name of the person who needs to request approval, then turn on Ask To Buy.

   Note: Age restrictions for Ask To Buy vary by region. In the United States, the family organizer can turn on Ask To Buy for any family member under age 18; for children under age 13, it's turned on by default.

Hide your purchases on iPad

With Family Sharing, you can hide your iTunes Store, App Store, and Apple Books purchases from family members.

1. Go to Settings ⚙ > [*your name*] > Family Sharing.

2. Tap Purchase Sharing, then turn off Share My Purchases.

Share subscriptions with family members on iPad

When you're in a Family Sharing group, you can share a subscription to Apple Music and Apple News+ with family members.

Use a shared Apple Music family membership

If your family has an Apple Music family membership, you can simply open Apple Music and start listening. If you don't have an Apple Music family membership, you can sign up for one.

Go to Settings > [your name] > Family Sharing.

Tap Apple Music, then follow the onscreen instructions.

Each family member gets their own music library and personal recommendations. (Selections are subject to content restrictions set in Screen Time.) To listen to music, make sure you're signed in with the Apple ID you entered in Family Sharing settings.

Use a shared Apple News+ subscription

In News, you can subscribe to Apple News+, which includes over 200 magazines and other publications. When you're in a Family Sharing group and you buy an Apple News+ subscription, all members of your family can read Apple News+ publications for no additional charge. The other members of your family get a message about Apple News+ when they open News. If you don't have a subscription, you can sign up through the News app (not available in all countries or regions).

Use a shared Apple Arcade subscription

Your family can share a subscription to Apple Arcade (not available in all countries or regions), a service that gives you access to new games without ads or additional purchases. With an Apple Arcade subscription, all members of your family (up to six people) can download and play Apple Arcade games from the App Store. (Selections are subject to content restrictions set in Screen Time.) The subscription allows you to play across iPhone, iPad, iPod touch, Mac, and Apple TV. Each player gets a personalized account—your progress is carried over between devices.

New games are added to Apple Arcade regularly. If you don't have a subscription, you can sign up for one through the App Store (not available in all countries or regions).

Share photos, a calendar, and more with family members on iPad

With Family Sharing on iPad, you can share a family photo album, a family calendar, your location, and more.

Share photos or videos with family members

When you set up Family Sharing, a shared album called Family is automatically created in the Photos app on all family members' devices, which makes it easy to share family photos or videos.

1. Open the Photos app 🌸, then select a photo or video, or select multiple photos or videos.

2. Tap 📤, then tap Shared Albums.

3. Add any comments you want, then tap Shared Albums.

4. Choose an album to add the photo or video to.

Members can unsubscribe from the family album, and the family organizer can delete it or remove subscribers.

Add an event to the family calendar

When you set up Family Sharing, a shared calendar called Family is automatically created in the Calendar app on all family members' devices. You can schedule an event on this calendar to share it with family members.

1. Open the Calendar app 🗓, then add an event.

2. While entering the event details, tap Calendar, then tap Family to add the event to the family calendar.

Members can unsubscribe from the family calendar, and the family organizer can delete it.

Share your location with family members

With Family Sharing, you can share your location with members of your family group. When the family organizer sets up Location Sharing in Family Sharing settings, the organizer's location is automatically shared with everyone in the family. Then family members can choose whether or not to share their location.

When you share your location, your family members can see your location in **Find My** on and in Messages and, if your device is lost, they can help you locate it with **Find My** on.

Note: To share your location, you must have Location Services turned on in Settings 🔘 > Privacy.

1. Go to Settings > [*your name*] > Family Sharing > Location Sharing, then turn on Share My Location.

2. Tap Change My Location to This iPad.

3. Tap a family member you want to share your location with, tap Share My Location, then tap ⟨.

You can repeat this step for each family member you want to share your location with. Each family member receives a message that you're sharing your location and can choose to share their location with you.

You can also send or share your location from the Messages app (iOS 8, iPadOS 13, or later) by tapping the profile picture or name at the top of the conversation, tapping , then tapping Send My Current Location or Share My Location.

To stop sharing your location with a family member, tap the profile picture or name at the top of the conversation with the family member, tap , then tap Stop Sharing My Location.

To find a family member's location, use the **Find My** on app .

Share a Personal Hotspot

With Family Sharing, you can share an Internet connection through a Personal Hotspot with members of your family group. When a member of your family group sets up a Personal Hotspot, other family members can use it without having to enter the password..

Locate a family member's missing device on iPad

When you're in a Family Sharing group and family members share their locations with you, you can use the Find My app ⊙ on your iPhone, iPad, or iPod touch, or on iCloud.com on a computer to help a family member find a lost device.

Set up your device to be found by a family member

A family member can help locate your missing device if you do the following on the device *before* it's lost:

- *Turn on Location Services:* Go to Settings ⚙ > Privacy, then turn on Location Services.

- *Turn on Find My iPad:* Go to Settings > [*your name*] > Find My > Find My iPad, then turn on Find My iPad, Enable Offline Finding, and Send Last Location.

- *Share your location with family members:* Go to Settings > [*your name*] > Family Sharing > Location

Sharing, then turn on Share My Location and make sure Find My iPad is turned on.

Locate a family member's device

1. Open Find My on your iPhone, iPad, or iPod touch, or open Find My iPhone on iCloud.com on a computer.

2. Sign in with your **Apple ID**.

3. In the list of devices, select the one you want to find.

   Your devices are at the top of the list, and your family members' devices are below yours.

   The selected device appears on a map so you can see where it is.

Set up Screen Time for family members on iPad

You can set up Screen Time for family members through Family Sharing—including downtime, allowances for app use, the contacts your family communicates with, content ratings, and more. Screen Time also lets you and your family members see how they're using their devices and use that information to structure their device use.

You can invite family members to join and enter their Apple IDs in Family Sharing on your device to begin the process. Or you can set up Screen Time for them in Family Sharing on your device.

Note*:* When you set up Screen Time for a family member through Family Sharing, notifications of your family member's weekly report appear on both your device and your family member's. To view the report, tap the notification.

1. Go to   Settings 🔘 >   [*your name*] > Family Sharing > Screen Time.

2. Tap a family member, then tap Turn on Screen Time.

3. Tap Continue, then follow the onscreen instructions.

   Important: If you set up Screen Time for a family member through Family Sharing and you forget the family Screen Time passcode, you can reset it on your device using your device passcode, Touch ID, or Face ID.

Chapter 7
QUICK Tips & Tricks:
Use Apple Pencil To Take Notes on Lock Screen

The new iPads support the first generation Apple Pencil. Go to Settings -> Notes and you can configure it to automatically launch a new note when you tap the iPad screen with your Apple Pencil on the Lock screen.

Close Multiple Tabs in Safari

Using Safari on the iPad is an amazing experience. But you do end up opening a lot of tabs quickly. Just tap and hold on the Tab Switcher button and tap on the Close All Tabs button to quickly close all open tabs.

Lock Notes

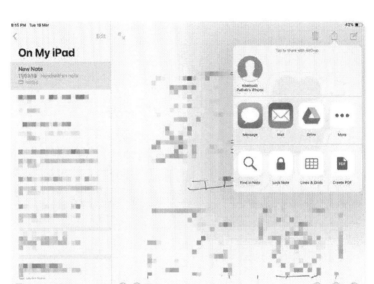

One of the lesser known features of Apple Notes is the ability to lock notes using Touch ID. Open a note, tap on the Share button and select Lock note to get started.

Use Screen Time to Monitor Time Spent

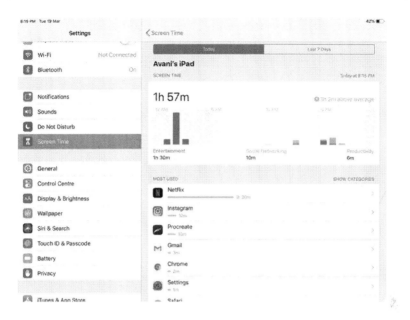

iOS 12 has an awesome new feature called Screen Time that tells you just how much time you're spending on your iPad and it breaks it down based on categories and app usage. Go to Settings -> Screen Time to enable the feature.

Set App Limits

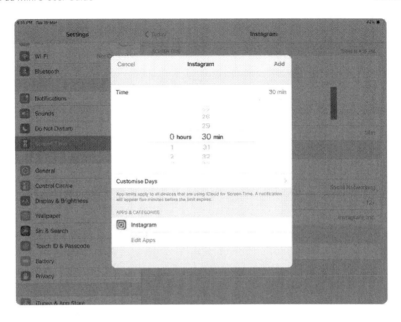

App Limits feature in Screen Time will help you fight your app addiction. If you find yourself spending too much time on Netflix or Facebook, go to Screen Time section, find the app and set an App Limit for it. Set it to be 30 minutes or 1 hour a day.

Move Multiple Apps Together on Home screen

The iPad Pro's home screen is very basic, but at least Apple has made it easier to move things around. You can tap and hold an app icon to put it in wiggle mode. Then drag one icon, so it's out of the grid. Now, with your other hand or finger, you can tap on more apps to add them to the pile of selected icons. Now, move the finger to another page or folder and release it to move all the selected app icons to the next place.

Use The Hidden Cursor Mode

When you have the software keyboard up, just tap and hold on the Space bar to turn the keyboard into a trackpad. Then you can swipe left, right, up or down to move the cursor in those directions. This gives you precise control over the cursor placement.

Enable AssistiveTouch

AssistiveTouch, which gives users a software home button is also available on the iPad. Go to Settings -> General -> Accessibility -> AssistiveTouch to enable it.

Once enabled, you can define double tap and tap and hold gestures for quick actions. The AssistiveTouch button expands when you tap it. You can configure 6 or more actions here as well.

Add Website To Home Screen

Some things still work better in Safari and negate the need to install a special app. In such a case, you can add websites as Home screen shortcuts. Open the website, tap on Share button and select Add to Home screen.

Use Shortcuts App For Automation

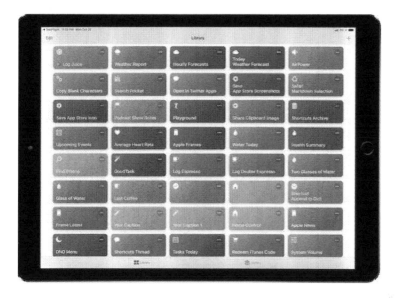

The A12 Bionic chip in the new iPad is a beast. There's no app on the App Store that will slow it down. But it still might not be a Laptop replacement because of the software.

The new Shortcuts app by Apple helps bridge some of the gaps. You can create automation workflows that will help you do things that apps on the App Store just can't.

Record Your iPad Screen

You can easily record your iPad screen to show a process to someone. Go to Settings -> Control Center -

> Customize Controls and turn on the Screen Recording toggle. Now, open the Control Center and tap Screen Recording toggle to start recording the screen (and the audio if you want).

How to Take a Screenshot

Use the Power and Home button at the same time to take a screenshot. Once a screenshot is taken, you'll see a preview of it in the bottom-left corner. You can tap on it to quickly edit it or share it.

Add Multiple Fingers to Touch ID

When you set up the iPad, you'll only have to add one finger to Touch ID. But you can go to Settings -> Touch ID to add more fingers. You can name individual fingers as well, making it easy to identify if you're sharing the iPad with multiple people.

Turn off keyboard clicks

The nasty keyboard click of iOS devices is one of the most annoying things you'll hear on public transport. Don't become part of the problem. As standard iOS devices are set to emit a clacky tap sound every time you hit a key no the virtual keyboard. To turn it off go to Settings > Sounds. You'll find the Keyboard Clicks slider right down at the bottom of the list there.

<h3 style="text-align:center">The Quickload bar</h3>

One of the Home screen's most important features is the quick-load bar – the dock of icons at the bottom of the screen. You can change what apps feature very easily. Hold down a finger on an app icon until it starts to jiggle. Then drag the app you want on the dock down to it. You can remove dock apps in the same way. Up to six apps can be stored in the quick-load dock.

Drag and Drop Files or Text Between Apps

Once you have two apps running side by side, you can drag and drop images, text, and files from one app to another.

Watch Videos in Picture in Picture

This feature is enabled by default. When you're watching a video in an app like Netflix, just hit the Home button. The video will continue to play in a small floating window. You can resize it and move it around.

New Way to Access Control Center

To access Control Center, swipe down from the right edge of the status bar.

Quick Gesture For App Switching

As the iPad Air support iPhone X and iPad Pro gestures, you can quickly switch between apps by using a small arc style gesture. Just swipe left to right, making a small semi-circle, and you'll be able to switch to the most recent app.

How to Reduce Your iPhone or iPad Network Data Usage With iPadOS's Low Data Mode

Apple understands that some iPhone and iPad users may prefer to keep tabs on their cellular network data usage, especially if they risk incurring charges by going over a certain limit.

The same goes for users who have a bandwidth cap on their broadband network, or anyone who regularly connects to a public Wi-Fi network that charges per megabyte.

That's why in iOS 13, Apple has included a Low Data Mode for apps that use cellular and Wi-Fi connections. The feature sends an explicit signal to apps to reduce their network data use by deferring non-compulsory tasks and disabling background app refresh.

To turn on the cellular or Wi-Fi setting on your iPhone or iPad, simply follow these steps.

How to Turn On Cellular Low Data Mode

- Launch the Settings app on your device

- Tap Cellular (or Mobile Data, depending on your region).

- Tap Cellular Data Options (or Mobile Data Options).

- Tap the Low Data Mode switch to toggle it to the green ON position.

How to Turn On Wi-Fi Low Data Mode

- Launch the Settings app on your device

- Tap Wi-Fi.

- Tap the info button (an encircled 'i' icon) alongside the Wi-Fi network in question.

- Tap the Low Data Mode switch to toggle it to the green ON position.

Note that a given third-party app must explicitly support Low Data Mode for there to be any change in its data usage, otherwise enabling the mode won't have any effect.

Quickly Access Spotlight From Anywhere

There's a huge advantage to using the iPad with a keyboard. Using the Command + Space shortcut, you can bring up Spotlight from anywhere. Start tying an app's name and if it's the first in the suggestions, just press Enter key to open it.

Use Apple Pencil to Take Notes on Lock Screen

The new iPads support the first generation Apple Pencil. Go to Settings -> Notes and you can configure it to automatically launch a new note when you tap the iPad screen with your Apple Pencil on the Lock screen.

Close Multiple Tabs in Safari

Using Safari on the iPad is an amazing experience. But you do end up opening a lot of tabs quickly. Just tap and hold on the Tab Switcher button and tap on the Close All Tabs button to quickly close all open tabs.

How to Mute Email Threads in iPadOS

When you're part of a busy group chat in a message app like WhatsApp, the notifications come fast, and can quickly become tiresome if you're not participating as actively as others in the same chat thread.

The same can be said for email conversation threads, especially ones where each message gets copied into multiple recipients. That's why in iOS 13, Apple has introduced an option to mute an email thread in the Mail app, so you don't get a notification every time a new email in that thread is received.

Using the mute feature in Apple Mail is easy – simply follow the steps below to enable it on the email thread in question.

- Launch the stock Mail app on your iPhone or iPad.

- Locate the email thread in your inbox that you would like to mute.

- Swipe left across the email and then tap More.

- Tap Mute from the pop-up menu.

A bell icon with a line through it will identify the email threads in your inbox that are muted. Note that you can unmute a muted thread just as easily by swiping left across it, tapping More, and then selecting Unmute.

Lock Notes

One of the lesser known features of Apple Notes is the ability to lock notes using Touch ID. Open a note, tap on the Share button and select Lock note to get started.

Use Screen Time to Monitor Time Spent

iOS 12 has an awesome new feature called Screen Time that tells you just how much time you're spending on your iPad and it breaks it down based on categories and app usage. Go to Settings -> Screen Time to enable the feature.

How to Block People From Sending You Mail in iPadOS

Unsolicited phone calls and text messages on your iPhone are annoying enough, but that frustration can quickly creep into your inbox when spammy messages start evading your junk email filters.

In iOS 13, Apple has thankfully recognized the stress this can cause users and has included a way for you to block specific email senders. The new feature draws from the blocked list in your contacts, and extends this to Apple's Mail app.

The steps below show you how to set up this option to prevent the same blocked contacts from reaching your inbox.

- First, make sure that the email address you want to block is linked to a contact in the Contacts app. To add an email to a selected contact, simply tap the Edit button and then tap the green plus symbol next to the email entry. Once you've entered it, hit Done.

- Next, launch the Settings app on your iPhone.

- Scroll down and tap Mail.

- Under the Threading options, tap the switch next to Ignore Blocked Senders to toggle it to the green ON position.

Note that directly below the Ignore Blocked Senders switch is an option to review the phone numbers on your blocked list and add new ones if desired.

Dictation keyboard

If you're tired of tapping away at the iPad virtual keyboard, you can also talk to it. When connected to a Wi-Fi network, a microphone button will appear on the bottom line of the virtual keyboard. Tap this, and you can freely talk to the iPad. The file will then be piped over to Apple's servers and translated – Siri-style.

How to use Favorites in Apple Maps

Apple Maps may not be your go-to map app at the moment, but iOS 13 could change that. Apple Maps in iOS 13 has been improved to include more roads, beaches, buildings, and other details. But the really cool additions are the new features. You can add locations to a Favorites list, and organize those saved locations into your own customized collections. To add a Favorite, tap on or search for a location, then scroll down the card and tap Add to Favorites. Your Favorite will then appear in your Favorites list on your main page.

To add a location to a collection, drag up from your main Apple Maps page, then tap on My Places > Add a Place. From there, you can add a recently viewed location to your collection, or search for it from the search bar. To start a new collection, head back to your main Apple Maps page, drag up from the bottom of the screen, then tap New Collection to create a new list.

How to use Look Around in Apple Maps

Look Around is Apple's answer to Google Streetview, and it allows you to "look around" a location before you visit. To use it, head to a location on Apple Maps and select it by long-pressing on the map. If Look Around is supported in this location you'll see a Look Around image. Tap it to jump down to street level and drag to move around. While you're here, you can also drag up from the bottom of the screen to see facts about the location, or add it to your Favorites.

Apple doesn't yet have the same coverage as Google, but it has promised to have the entire U.S. covered by the end of 2019, with other countries following afterwards.

How to use the Find My app

Apple has combined Find My Friends and Find My iPhone into the imaginatively named app, Find My. This addition to iOS 13 allows you to share your location with friends and loved ones, and find your devices from the same app.

It's simple to use. Launch the Find My app from your home page and it'll show your current location in the People tab. To share with a contact, press the Start Sharing Location button and type in whichever contact you want to share your location with. To find a lost device, hit the Devices tab to change your map to show all the Apple devices registered with your account. Tap on an individual device to Play Sound, get Directions to your device, Mark As Lost, or remotely Erase This Device. If one of your devices is offline, you can ask

Find My to alert you when it's back online by hitting Notify Me.

How to change wallpapers

You've been able to choose your wallpaper within iOS for some time now, and it's the best way to put your stamp on your iPad. To change the wallpaper go to Settings > Brightness & Wallpaper and tap the images of your current wallpaper. You'll then be able to choose your image from the image gallery.

How to use Swipe Typing

In iOS 13 Apple is also adding Swipe Typing to iOS's default keyboard. Long loved by many Android users, this mode allows you to swipe your finger across your keyboard's keys to type a word instead of tapping out each character. While it can take some getting used to, once figured out, it's generally thought to be a faster way of typing than tapping.

There's no need to switch this option on — it's on by default, and you can use it by just dragging your finger across your keyboard.

How to use Cycle Tracking in Health

Apple's Health app is a powerful tool, and it's seeing some amazing additions in iPadOS 13 — the biggest of which is probably Cycle Tracking. This allows you to track your menstrual cycles, and includes tools to let you know when you're due or at your most fertile.

To get started, open your Health app and select Search and then select Cycle Tracking from the list. Tap that and hit Get Started > Next. The app will then ask you a couple of questions, including when your last period began, and how long they usually last. You'll also be given options on how you would like to track your period, and can choose to be given predictions and notifications on when your next period is likely to begin, whether you would like to log symptoms and spotting in your Cycle Log, and whether you want to be shown your windows of fertility.

Once you've answered the app's questions, you'll be sent back to the Cycle Tracking homepage. From here, you can tap Add Period to select days on which you've experienced your period, or you can go into

172

more detail by tapping the Flow Level, Symptoms, and Spotting options to log those specifics.

Switch off location services

Everyone knowing your location is one of the most legitimate "paranoid" concerns of the modern tech age. Plenty of iPad apps pinpoint you to a location, and will even make this public knowledge at times. You can turn this feature off if you're worried, within Settings > Privacy. You'll see the Location Services options at the top of this sub-menu.

Check out the Privacy menu to keep control

The iOS 6 software at the heart of the iPad keeps track of all the apps that ask for data from other apps – most often things like your calendar or your Twitter account. You can see which apps are trying to access this data in Settings > Privacy. Unless you're downloading some seriously low-rent apps, you shouldn't find anything to worry about, though.

Alerts and notifications

If you find that your iPad is bothering you a bit too much, you can turn off notifications for certain apps. This will come in particularly handy if you play free-to-play games – which are generally incessant naggers. Each of your apps gets an entry in the Settings > Notifications menu. You can select whether updates show up, how they appear and whether they pop-up on your lock screen or not.

How to edit photos and rotate videos

While there are third-party editing apps for iOS, the base iPhone software has always lacked its own editing tools. That is, until iOS 13. Now you can adjust various key parts of your photos and videos from your Photos app. To give it a go for yourself, head into your Photos app. From there, select a photo and then tap the Edit button. From there, try swiping between options and adjusting sliders to see how altering various options changes the look of your picture.

Many of these editing options are also available for videos, and you can now rotate videos with the Photos app.

Setting a profile picture in iMessage

Say goodbye to "new phone, who is this?" texts, as iMessage now allows you to set a profile image and screen name that's shared with selected contacts. So now, when you text a fellow iPhone user, you can let them know exactly who's texting without them needing to save your contact information.

It's easy to set up. First, open Messages, tap the three dots ("…") in the top-right corner, and hit Edit Name and Photo. From here, you can type in a preferred first and last name, and set a profile picture. You can select to use your personal Memoji as a profile picture, or you can select from a variety of Animojis instead. You can also change whether you want to share this information with Contacts Only, Anyone, or to Always Ask if the information is to be shared.

Do Not Disturb

For an even more carefree life, there's Do Not Disturb. This is a mode that stops all notifications. It's perfect if you fancy an afternoon snooze and don't want to be awoken by the bleat of an attention-seeking iPad. The

Do Not Disturb mode slider can be found towards the top of the Settings menu.

How to Disable Apple Music Listening History On iPad

One of the primary benefits to disabling this feature, especially on iPad, is if you share your iPad between multiple users. This way, Apple Music suggestions don't get confused or jumbled up due to multiple users requesting music at the same time. Learn how to disable this feature.

- Open the Settings app.
- Scroll down until you see Music and tap on it.
- Scroll down until you see Use Listening History.
- Switch the toggle off.

Now, when you play music through the HomePod; it will no longer use it against your listening history, giving you a better overall experience until Apple adds voice profiles.

How to Customize Your Animoji and Memoji

Speaking of Memojis and Animojis, you no longer need an iPhone with TrueDepth technology (either the iPhone X, XS, XS Max, or XR) to create a Memoji in iOS 13. While you'll still need a TrueDepth camera to have your Memoji or Animoji follow your movements, owners of the iPhone 6S or newer on iOS 13 will also be able to make their own Memoji. Just head into iMessage, open a conversation, and hit the Memoji icon, followed by the "+" button.

How to share music over AirPods

One of the coolest new additions to iOS 13 is the option to have the same music stream across two pairs of AirPods. To get going, you'll need to pair the second pair of AirPods with your iPhone. Once you've done that, you'll be able to select the second pair of AirPods from your AirPlay settings in the same way you can select your own.

How to save your passwords

Much like iOS 12, you can save your passwords and logins to your iCloud Keychain in iOS 13. You will be asked if you want to save login information to the iCloud Keychain whenever you log into a service, but if you want to manually manage your details, you can do so by heading to Settings > Passwords & Accounts > Website & App Passwords. You may need to use Touch ID, Face ID, or your passcode to log into this screen.

Using Screen Time and setting app limits

If you're an iOS 12 veteran, then it's likely you've spent some time with Screen Time already. But if you haven't, it's simple to set up it up to help you keep an eye on how much you're using your iPhone. To get started with Screen Time, just go to Settings > Screen Time.

If you really want to go ham on your usage, then you can set limits for how long you can use specific apps with Screen Time's App Limits feature. To do this, head to Settings > Screen Time > App Limits, and then tap Add Limit. In a change from iOS 12, you can now specify apps within a category and group them together in the same limit. So you can limit yourself to a combined total of seven hours a day on Fortnite, Twitter, and Spotify if you want to. Once a limit is reached, a splash screen will let you know and give you the opportunity to ignore the limit for either the whole day, or just another 15 minutes.

Tap the Title Bar

Have you ever scrolled down a long list or been at the bottom of a large web page and needed to get back to the top? There's no need to scroll. Most of the time, you can tap the title bar of the app or web page to return to the beginning of the list. This works with most apps and most web pages, although not every web page is designed to be iPad-friendly.

Skip the Apostrophe

Skipping the apostrophe is also a great time-saver and ranks as my number one keyboard tip. This secret relies on auto-correct to do some of the typing for us. The auto-correct feature on the iPad can be quite annoying, but at times, it can also save you some time.

The coolest trick is the ability to insert an apostrophe for most contractions like 'can't' and 'won't.' Simply type the words without the apostrophe, and autocorrect will usually insert it for you.

You can also use the predictive typing suggestions that appear at the top of the keyboard to help speed up your typing, and if you don't like the on-screen keyboard, you can install a third-party keyboard from companies like Google or Grammarly.

The Virtual Touchpad

Possibly the number one thing people miss about their PC is the mouse. The ability to tell your computer what to do by touching the screen is great for ordinary uses, but when you want to do a lot of typing, the ability to move the cursor with a touchpad or mouse is... well, there are few substitutes.

This might be why Apple added a virtual touchpad to the iPad's on-screen keyboard. This often overlooked secret can make a world of distance if you frequently create long messages or lists using the iPad. Simply hold two or more fingers down on the on-screen keyboard and move your fingers without lifting them from the display and a cursor within the text will move with your fingers.

Open Apps and Find Music and Quickly Using Spotlight Search

Did you know the iPad has a universal search feature? There's no need to go hunting through pages and pages of apps for just the right one, and no reason to open music just to play a song. Spotlight Search can find anything from music to videos to contacts to apps on your device. It will even suggest websites to visit.

You can launch Spotlight Search by swiping down with your finger while you are on the Home Screen, which is the name of the screen with all of your apps on it. Any time you are on the Home Screen (i.e., not inside an app or using Siri), you can swipe down to initiate a Spotlight Search. The key here is to swipe down somewhere in the middle of the screen. If you swipe from the very top of the display, you will open the Notification Center.

The great thing about Spotlight Search is that it searches your entire device, so you can even use it to search for a specific text message or email. It will even search through Notes. You can turn on and off different results through the general settings of your iPad under Spotlight Search.

Chapter 8

How to use the Accessibility features

Get started with accessibility features on iPad.

iPad provides many accessibility features to support your vision, physical and motor, hearing, and learning needs. Learn how to configure these features and set up shortcuts for easy access.

Turn on accessibility features during setup

You can turn on many accessibility features right away when you first set up iPad. Turn on iPad, then do any of the following:

- *Turn on VoiceOver:* Triple-click the top button (iPad Pro (11-inch) and iPad Pro (12.9-inch) (3rd generation)) or triple-click the Home button (other models).

- *Turn on Zoom:* Double-tap the screen with three fingers.

- *Turn on Switch Control, Larger Text, Smart Invert, and more:* Choose a language and country, tap 🔵 , then choose the features you want.

Change accessibility settings

After you set up iPad, you can adjust accessibility settings.

1. Go to Settings ⚙️ > Accessibility.

2. Choose any of the following features:

  - Vision

    - VoiceOver

    - Zoom

    - Magnifier

    - Display & Text Size

    - Motion

    - Spoken Content

    - Audio Descriptions

  - Physical and Motor

    - Touch

    - Face ID & Attention

- Switch Control

- Voice Control

- Home or top button

- Apple TV Remote

- Keyboards

- Apple Pencil

- Hearing

  - Hearing Devices

  - RTT

  - Audio/Visual

  - Subtitles & Captioning

- General

  - Guided Access

  - Siri

  - Accessibility Shortcut

Turn on and practice VoiceOver on iPad

With VoiceOver—a gesture-based screen reader—you can
use iPad even if you don't see the screen. VoiceOver gives

audible descriptions of what's on your screen—from battery level, to who's calling, to which app your finger is on. You can also adjust the speaking rate and pitch to suit your needs.

When you touch the screen or drag your finger over it, VoiceOver speaks the name of the item your finger is on, including icons and text. To interact with the item, such as a button or link, or to navigate to another item, use VoiceOver gestures.

When you go to a new screen, VoiceOver plays a sound, then selects and speaks the name of the first item on the screen (typically in the top-left corner). VoiceOver tells you when the display changes to landscape or portrait orientation, when the screen becomes dimmed or locked, and what's active on the Lock screen when you wake iPad.

Turn VoiceOver on or off

Important: VoiceOver changes the gestures you use to control iPad. When VoiceOver is on, you must use VoiceOver gestures to operate iPad.

To turn VoiceOver on or off, use any of the following methods:

- Go to Settings ⚙ > Accessibility > VoiceOver, then turn the setting on or off.

- **Summon Siri** and say "Turn on VoiceOver" or "Turn off VoiceOver."

- **Triple-click the Home button** (models with the Home button).

- **Triple-click the top button** (other models).

- Use Control Center.

Learn and practice VoiceOver gestures

You can practice VoiceOver gestures in a special area without affecting iPad or its settings. When you practice a gesture, VoiceOver describes the gesture and the resulting action.

Try different techniques to discover which works best for you. If a gesture doesn't work, try a quicker movement, especially for a double-tap or swipe gesture. To swipe, try brushing the screen quickly with your finger or fingers.

For best results using multifinger gestures, touch the screen with some space between your fingers.

1. Go to Settings ⚙ > Accessibility > VoiceOver.

2. Turn on VoiceOver, tap VoiceOver Practice, then double-tap to start.

3. Practice the following gestures with one, two, three, and four fingers:

   • Tap

   • Double-tap

   • Triple-tap

   • Swipe left, right, up, or down

   When you finish practicing, tap Done, then double-tap to exit.

Change your VoiceOver settings on iPad

You can customize the settings for VoiceOver, such as the audio options, language, voice, speaking rate, and verbosity.

Adjust the VoiceOver volume and other audio options

- To increase or decrease the volume, press the volume buttons on iPad.

- To set other audio options, go to Settings ⚙ > Accessibility > VoiceOver > Audio, then do any of the following:

  - Turn on Mute Sound Effects.

  - Turn on Audio Ducking to temporarily reduce playback volume when VoiceOver speaks.

  - Adjust audio routing options when you connect additional devices, such as an instrument amplifier or a DJ mixer.

Set the VoiceOver language

VoiceOver uses the same language you choose for your iPad. VoiceOver pronunciation of some languages is affected by the Region Format you choose.

1. Go to Settings ⚙ > General > Language & Region.

2. Tap iPad Language, then choose a language.

Adjust the speaking voice

Go to Settings 🔘 > Accessibility > VoiceOver, then do any of the following:

- *Adjust the speaking rate:* Drag the Speaking Rate slider.

- *Choose a voice:* Tap Speech > Voice, then choose a voice. To download an enhanced voice, tap ⬇.

- *Adjust the pitch:* Tap Speech, then drag the slider. You can also turn on Use Pitch Change to have VoiceOver use a higher pitch when speaking the first item of a group (such as a list or table) and a lower pitch when speaking the last item of a group.

- *Specify the pronunciation of certain words:* Tap Speech > Pronunciations, tap ✛, enter a phrase, then dictate or spell out how you want the phrase to be pronounced.

  Note: You can dictate only if you turned on Enable Dictation in Settings > General > Keyboards.

Set how much VoiceOver tells you

Go to Settings 🔘 > Accessibility > VoiceOver, then tap any of the following:

- *Verbosity:* Choose options to have VoiceOver speak hints, punctuation, uppercase letters, embedded links, and more. VoiceOver can even confirm rotor actions.

  To change how VoiceOver speaks punctuation, tap Punctuation, then choose a group. You can also create new groups—for example, a programming group in which "[" is spoken as "left brack."

- *Always   Speak Notifications:* VoiceOver   reads notifications, including incoming text messages as they occur, even if iPad is locked. Unacknowledged notifications are repeated when you unlock iPad.

Customize VoiceOver settings for an activity

You can customize a group of VoiceOver settings for an activity such as programming. Apply the settings automatically when you open certain apps or by adjusting the rotor.

1. Go   to Settings 🔘 >   Accessibility >   VoiceOver > Activities.

2. Choose an existing activity or tap Add Activity.

3. Adjust settings for speech, verbosity, and braille.

4. Choose Apps or Context to automatically apply the settings for this activity.

Adjust VoiceOver visuals

Go to Settings ⚙ > Accessibility > VoiceOver, then turn on any of the following:

- *Large Cursor:* If you have trouble seeing the black outline around the selected item, you can enlarge and thicken the outline.

- *Caption Panel:* The text spoken by VoiceOver is displayed at the bottom of the screen.

Learn VoiceOver gestures on iPad

When VoiceOver is on, standard touchscreen gestures have different effects, and additional gestures let you move around the screen and control individual items. VoiceOver gestures include two-, three-, and four-finger taps and swipes.

You can use different techniques to perform VoiceOver gestures. For example, you can perform a two-finger tap using two fingers on one hand, one finger on each hand, or your thumbs. Instead of selecting an item and double-tapping, you can use a split-tap gesture—touch and hold an item with one finger, then tap the screen with another finger.

Explore and speak items on the screen

To explore the screen, drag your finger over it. VoiceOver speaks the name of each item you touch.

You can also use VoiceOver gestures to explore the screen in order, from top to bottom and left to right.

Operate iPad using VoiceOver gestures

When VoiceOver is on, you need to use special gestures to unlock iPad, go to the Home screen, open Control Center, switch apps, and more.

Unlock iPad

- **Models with Face ID**: Wake iPad and glance at it, then drag up from the bottom edge of the screen until you hear two rising tones.

- **Models with Touch ID**: Press the Home button.

- **Other models**: Press the Home button, then enter your passcode.

To avoid having your passcode spoken as you enter it, enter your passcode silently using handwriting mode or type onscreen braille.

Go to the Home screen

- Drag one finger up from the bottom edge of the screen until you hear two rising tones, then lift your finger.

- Press the Home button (models with the Home button).

Use the dock

- Slide one finger up from the bottom edge until you hear two rising tones, then swipe down.

- Switch to another app

- Swipe right or left with five fingers to cycle through the open apps. (Make sure Gestures is turned on in Settings ⚙ > General > Multitasking & Dock.)

Alternatively, you can use the App Switcher:

1. Open the App Switcher using one of the following methods:

- Drag one finger up from the bottom edge of the screen until you hear three tones, then lift your finger.

- Double-click the Home button (models with the Home button).

To browse the open apps, swipe left or right until the app you want is selected.

Double-tap to open the app.

Open Control Center

- Drag one finger down from the top edge of the screen until you hear two rising tones.

- Tap any item in the status bar, then swipe up with three fingers.

To dismiss Control Center, do a two-finger scrub.

View notifications

- Drag one finger down from the top edge of the screen until you hear three rising tones.

- Tap any item in the status bar, then swipe down with three fingers.

To dismiss the notifications screen, do a two-finger scrub.

Speak status bar information

1. Tap the status bar at the top of the screen.

2. Swipe left or right to hear the time, battery state, Wi-Fi signal strength, and more.

Rearrange apps on your Home screen

Use one of the following methods:

- *Drag and drop:* Tap an icon on the Home screen, then double-tap and hold your finger on the screen until you hear three rising tones. The item's relative location is described as you drag. Lift your finger when the icon is in its new location. Drag an icon to the edge of the screen to move it to another Home screen.

- *Move actions:* Tap an app, then swipe down to hear available actions. When you hear "Edit Mode," double-tap to start arranging apps. Find the app you want to move, then swipe down to the Move action and double-tap. Move the VoiceOver cursor to the new destination for the app, then choose from the available actions: Cancel Move, Create New Folder, Add to Folder, Move Before, or Move After.

When you're finished, tap Done, then double-tap.

Search from the Home screen

1. Tap anywhere on the Home screen outside the status bar.

2. Swipe down with three fingers.

Control VoiceOver using the rotor on iPad

You can use the VoiceOver rotor to change how VoiceOver works. You can adjust the VoiceOver volume or speaking rate, move from one item to the next on the screen, select special input methods such as Braille Screen Input or Handwriting, and more.

When you use Magic Keyboard to control VoiceOver, use the rotor to adjust settings such as volume, speech rate, use of pitch or phonetics, typing echo, and reading of punctuation.

Use the VoiceOver rotor

1. When VoiceOver is turned on, rotate two fingers on your screen as if you're turning a dial. If you prefer to use one finger on each hand, simultaneously drag up with one finger and drag down with the other.

   VoiceOver speaks the rotor setting. Keep rotating your fingers to hear more settings. Stop rotating your fingers when you hear the setting you want.

2. Swipe your finger up or down on the screen to use the setting.

   The available rotor settings and their effects depend on what you're doing. For example, if you choose Headings when you're browsing a webpage, a swipe down or up will move the VoiceOver cursor to the next or previous heading.

Customize the VoiceOver rotor

1. Go to Settings ⚙ > Accessibility > VoiceOver.

2. Do any of the following:

   - *Add or reorder the rotor settings:* Tap Rotor, then choose the settings you want, or drag ≡ to reorder settings.

- *Add another language:* Tap Speech > Add New Language (below Rotor Languages), then choose a language.

- *Have VoiceOver confirm rotor actions:* Tap Verbosity, then turn on Speak Confirmation.

Use the onscreen keyboard with VoiceOver on iPad

VoiceOver changes how you use the onscreen keyboard when you activate an editable text field. You can enter, select, and delete text; change the keyboard language; and more.

Enter text with the onscreen keyboard

1. Select a text field, then double-tap.

   The insertion point and the onscreen keyboard appear.

2. Enter text using one of the following methods:

   - *Standard typing (default):* Select a key on the keyboard by swiping left or right, then double-tap to enter the character. Or move your finger around the keyboard to select a key and, while continuing to touch the key with one finger, tap the screen with another finger. VoiceOver speaks the key when it's selected, and again when the character is entered.

- *Touch typing:* Touch a key on the keyboard to select it, then lift your finger to enter the character. If you touch the wrong key, slide your finger to the key you want. VoiceOver speaks the character for each key as you touch it, but doesn't enter a character until you lift your finger.

- *Direct Touch typing:* VoiceOver is disabled for the keyboard only, so you can type just as you do when VoiceOver is off.

- *Dictation:* Use a two-finger double-tap on the keyboard to start and stop dictation.

To enter an accented character, use one of the following methods:

- *Standard typing (default):* Select the plain character, then double-tap and hold until you hear a tone indicating alternate characters have appeared. Drag left or right to select and hear the choices. Release your finger to enter the current selection.

- *Touch typing:* Touch and hold a character until the alternate characters appear.

Edit text with the onscreen keyboard

- *Move the insertion point:* Swipe up or down to move the insertion point forward or backward in the text. Use the rotor to choose whether you want to move the insertion point by character, by word, or by line. To jump to the beginning or end, double-tap the text.

  VoiceOver makes a sound when the insertion point moves, and speaks the character, word, or line that the insertion point moves across. When moving forward by words, the insertion point is placed at the end of each word, before the space or punctuation that follows. When moving backward, the insertion point is placed at the end of the preceding word, before the space or punctuation that follows it.

- *Move the insertion point past the punctuation at the end of a word or sentence:* Use the rotor to switch back to character mode.

  When moving the insertion point by line, VoiceOver speaks each line as you move across it. When moving forward, the insertion point is placed at the beginning of the next line (except when you reach the last line of a paragraph, when the insertion point is moved to the end of the line just spoken). When moving backward, the insertion point is placed at the beginning of the line that's spoken.

- *Delete a character:* Use ⌫.

- *Select text:* Use one of the following methods.

    - Set the rotor to Text Selection, swipe up or down to choose Character, Word, Line, or Sentence, then swipe left or right to move backward or forward. (You may need to enable Text Selection—go to Settings ⚙ > Accessibility > VoiceOver > Rotor.)

    - Set the rotor to Edit, swipe up or down to choose Select or Select All, then double-tap. If you choose Select, the word closest to the insertion point is selected when you double-tap. To increase or decrease the selection, **do a two-finger scrub** to dismiss the pop-up menu, then pinch.

Cut, copy, or paste: Set the rotor to Edit, select the text, swipe up or down to choose Cut, Copy, or Paste, then double-tap.

Fix misspelled words: Set the rotor to Misspelled Words, then swipe up or down to jump to the previous or next misspelled word. Swipe left or right to choose a suggested replacement, then double-tap to use the replacement.

Undo: Shake iPad, swipe left or right to choose the action to undo, then double-tap.

Change the keyboard settings

1. Go to Settings ⚙ > Accessibility > VoiceOver.

2. Tap any of the following:

   - *Typing Style:* You can choose a new style. Or, set the rotor to Typing Mode, then swipe up or down.

   - *Phonetic Feedback:* Speak text character by character. VoiceOver first speaks the character, then its phonetic equivalent—for example, "f" and then "foxtrot.

- *Typing Feedback:* Choose to speak characters, words, both, or nothing.

- *Rotor:* Select the settings you want to include in the rotor.

- *Speech:* Tap Add New Language (below Rotor Languages), then choose a language.

- *Verbosity:* Tap Deleting Text. To have VoiceOver speak deleted characters in a lower pitch, tap Change Pitch.

Write with your finger using VoiceOver on iPad

With Handwriting mode, you can enter text by writing characters on the screen with your finger. In addition to normal text entry, use handwriting mode to enter your iPad passcode silently or to open apps from the Home screen.

Use handwriting mode

1. Set the rotor to Handwriting.

   If Handwriting isn't in the rotor, go to Settings ⚙ > Accessibility > VoiceOver > Rotor, then add it.

2. To choose a character type (lowercase, numbers, uppercase, or punctuation), swipe up or down with three fingers.

   To hear the selected character type, tap with three fingers.

3. Trace a character on the screen with your finger.

   You can also do any of the following:

   - *Enter an alternate character (a character with an accent, for example):* Write the character, then swipe up or down with two fingers until you hear the type of character you want.

   - *Enter a space:* Swipe right with two fingers.

   - *Go to a new line:* Swipe right with three fingers.

   - *Delete the previous character:* Swipe left with two fingers.

   To exit handwriting mode, do a two-finger scrub, or set the rotor to a different setting.

Enter your passcode silently with handwriting mode

1. On the passcode screen, set the rotor to Handwriting.

2. Write the characters of your passcode with your finger.

Select an item on the Home screen

1. On the Home screen, set the rotor to Handwriting.

2. Start writing the name of the item with your finger.

   If there are multiple matches, continue to spell the name until it's unique, or swipe up or down with two fingers to choose from the current matches.

Quickly navigate a long list

1. Select the index to the right of the list (for example, next to your Contacts list or in the VoiceOver Item Chooser).

2. Set the rotor to Handwriting, then use your finger to write the letter you want to navigate to.

Control VoiceOver on iPad with Magic Keyboard

If you pair Magic Keyboard with iPad, you can use keyboard shortcuts on Magic Keyboard to activate VoiceOver commands.

Additionally, you can use VoiceOver Help to learn the keyboard layout and the actions associated with various key combinations. VoiceOver Help speaks keys and keyboard commands as you type them, without performing the associated action.

Choose the VoiceOver modifier

The modifier is a key or set of keys you press with one or more other keys to enter VoiceOver commands. You can set the modifier to be the Caps Lock key or the Control and Option keys pressed at the same time.

1. Go to Settings ⚙ > Accessibility > VoiceOver > Modifier Keys.

2. Choose the modifier for VoiceOver commands: the Caps Lock key or the Control and Option keys.

   This modifier is abbreviated as "VO" in the lists below.

VoiceOver keyboard commands

VO = modifier keys

- *Turn on VoiceOver Help:* VO-K

- *Turn off VoiceOver Help:* Esc (Escape)

- *Select the next or previous item:* VO-Right Arrow or VO-Left Arrow

- *Activate the selected item:* VO-Space bar

- *Touch and hold the selected item:* VO-Shift-M

- *Read from the current position:* VO-A

- *Read from the top:* VO-B

- *Pause or resume reading:* Control

- *Copy the last spoken text to the clipboard:* VO-Shift-C

- *Search for text:* VO-F

- *Mute or unmute VoiceOver:* VO-S

- *Go to the Home screen:* VO-H

- *Move to the status bar:* VO-M

- *Open the notifications screen:* Move to the status bar (VO-M), then Option-Up Arrow

- *Open Control Center:* Move to the status bar (VO-M), then Option-Down Arrow

- *Open Spotlight Search:* Option-Up Arrow

- *Open the App Switcher:* VO-H-H

- *Switch apps:* Command-Tab or Command-Shift-Tab

- *Open the Item Chooser:* VO-I

- *Change the label of the selected item:* VO-/

- *Start, stop, or pause an action:* VO-Hyphen

- *Swipe up or down:* VO-Up Arrow or VO-Down Arrow

- *Adjust the rotor:* VO-Command-Left Arrow or VO-Command-Right Arrow

- *Adjust the setting specified by the rotor:* VO-Command-Up Arrow or VO-Command-Down Arrow

- *Turn the screen curtain on or off:* VO-Shift-F11

- *Return to the previous screen:* Esc

Quick Nav using the arrow keys

Turn on Quick Nav to control VoiceOver using the arrow keys.

- *Turn Quick Nav on or off:* Left Arrow-Right Arrow

- *Select the next or previous item:* Right Arrow or Left Arrow

- *Select the next or previous item specified by the rotor:* Up Arrow or Down Arrow

- *Select the first or last item:* Control-Up Arrow or Control-Down Arrow

- *Tap an item:* Up Arrow-Down Arrow

- *Scroll up, down, left, or right:* Option-Up Arrow, Option-Down Arrow, Option-Left Arrow, or Option-Right Arrow

- *Adjust the rotor:* Up Arrow-Left Arrow or Up Arrow-Right Arrow

Single-key Quick Nav for web browsing

When you view a webpage with Quick Nav on, you can use the following keys on the keyboard to navigate the page quickly. Typing the key moves to the next item of the indicated type. To move to the previous item, hold the Shift key as you type the letter.

- *Turn on Single-key Quick Nav:* VO-Q

- *Heading:* H

- *Link:* L

- *Text field:* R

- *Button:* B

- *Form control:* C

- *Image:* I

- *Table:* T

- *Static text:* S

- *ARI   landmark:* W

- *List:* X

- *Item of the same type:* M

- *Level 1 heading:* 1

- *Level 2 heading:* 2

- *Level 3 heading:* 3

- *Level 4 heading:* 4

- *Level 5 heading:* 5

- *Level   heading:* 6

Text editing

Use these commands (with Quick Nav turned off) to work with text. VoiceOver reads the text as you move the insertion point.

- *Go forward or back one character:* Right Arrow or Left Arrow

211

- *Go forward or back one word:* Option-Right Arrow or Option-Left Arrow

- *Go up or down one line:* Up Arrow or Down Arrow

- *Go to the beginning or end of the line:* Command-Left Arrow or Command-Down Arrow

- *Go to the beginning or end of the paragraph:* Option-Up Arrow or Option-Down Arrow

- *Go to the previous or next paragraph:* Option-Up Arrow or Option-Down Arrow

- *Go to the top or bottom of the text field:* Command-Up Arrow or Command-Down Arrow

- *Select text as you move:* Shift + any of the insertion point movement commands above

- *Select all text:* Command-A

- *Copy, cut, or paste the selected text:* Command-C, Command-X, or Command-V

- *Undo or redo last change:* Command-Z or Shift-Command-Z

Type onscreen braille using VoiceOver on iPad

212

If you turn on Braille Screen Input, you can use your fingers to enter six-dot braille or contracted braille directly on the iPad screen.

Enter braille on the screen

Enter braille with iPad lying flat in front of you (tabletop mode), or hold iPad with the screen facing away so your fingers curl back to tap the screen (screen away mode).

1. Set the rotor to Braille Screen Input.

   If you don't see Braille Screen Input in the rotor, go to Settings ⚙ > Accessibility > VoiceOver > Rotor, then select it from the list.

2. Enter braille characters by tapping the screen with one or several fingers at the same time.

   You can also do any of the following:

   - *Enter a space:* Swipe right with one finger. (In screen away mode, swipe to *your* right.)

   - *Delete the previous character:* Swipe left with one finger.

   - *Move to a new line:* Swipe right with two fingers.

213

- *Cycle through spelling suggestions:* Swipe up or down with one finger.

- *Enter a carriage return, or send a message (in Messages):* Swipe up with three fingers.

- *Switch between six-dot braille and contracted braille:* Swipe to the right with three fingers.

- *Turn braille contractions on or off:* Swipe to the right with three fingers.

- *Translate immediately (when contractions are enabled):* Swipe down with two fingers.

- *Switch to the next keyboard:* Swipe up with two fingers.

To exit Braille Screen Input, do a two-finger scrub, or adjust the rotor to another setting.

Tip: To have iPad read dots aloud, tap and hold the dots, then when you hear the timer tones and announcement, release the dots.

Adjust entry dot positions

To move the entry dots to match your natural finger positions, double-tap all the dots.

214

Change Braille Screen Input settings

1. Go to Settings ⚙ > Accessibility > VoiceOver > Braille > Braille Screen Input.

2. Do any of the following:

   • Set six-dot or contracted Braille as the default.

   • Reverse dot positions for six-dot and eight-dot Braille.

Use a braille display with VoiceOver on iPad

You can use a Bluetooth braille display to read VoiceOver output, and a braille display with input keys and other controls to control iPad when VoiceOver is turned on

Connect a braille display

1. Turn on the braille display.

2. On iPad, go to Settings ⚙ > Bluetooth, turn on Bluetooth, then choose the display.

3. On iPad, go to Settings > Accessibility > VoiceOver > Braille, then choose the display.

Adjust the braille settings

1. On iPad, go to Settings ⚙ > Accessibility > VoiceOver > Braille.

2. Do any of the following:

   - Choose contracted, uncontracted eight-dot, or uncontracted six-dot braille input or output

   - Add Braille tables that appear in the Braille Table rotor

   - Turn on the status cell and choose its location

   - Turn on Nemeth code for mathematical equations

   - Display the onscreen keyboard

   - Choose to have the page turned automatically when panning

   - Change the braille translation from Unified English

   - Change the alert display duration

   - Adjust the key debounce duration (the timing used between typing and activating commands)

Output closed captions in braille during media playback

1. On   iPad,   go   to Settings ⚙ >   Accessibility >
VoiceOver > Verbosity.

2. Choose Braille or Speech and Braille.

Customize VoiceOver gestures and keyboard shortcuts on iPad

You can customize the gestures and keyboard shortcuts
that activate VoiceOver commands.

1. Go   to Settings ⚙ >   Accessibility >   VoiceOver >
Commands.

2. Tap any of the following:

- *All Commands:* Navigate to the command you want
  to customize, then tap Edit, Add Gesture, or Add
  Keyboard Shortcut.

- *Touch Gestures:* List   the   gestures   and   the
  associated commands.

- *Handwriting:* List the gestures for handwriting and
  the associated commands.

- *Braille Screen Input:* List the gestures for Braille
  Screen Input and the associated commands.

To clear your custom gestures and keyboard shortcuts, tap Reset VoiceOver Commands.

Use VoiceOver in apps on iPad

You can use VoiceOver to interact with apps such as Maps, Camera, Photos, Voice Memos, Safari, and more even if you can't see the screen.

Read PDF documents in Apple Books or Files using VoiceOver

VoiceOver can read detailed information—such as forms, tables, and lists—in PDF documents.

Browse the web in Safari using VoiceOver

- *Search the web:* Select the search field, double-tap to invoke the keyboard, enter your search, then swipe right or left to move down or up the list of suggested search phrases. Then double-tap the screen to search the web using the selected phrase.

- *Skip to the next page element of a particular type:* Set the rotor to the element type—such as headings, links, and form controls—then swipe up or down.

- *Set the rotor settings for web browsing:* Go to Settings ⚙ > Accessibility > VoiceOver > Rotor. Tap to select or deselect settings, or drag ☰ up or down to reposition an item.

- *Skip images while navigating:* Go to Settings > Accessibility > VoiceOver > Navigate Images. You can choose to skip all images or only those without descriptions.

- *Reduce page clutter for easier reading and navigation:* Select the Reader item in the Safari address field (not available for all webpages).

- *Allow websites to customize their behavior for assistive technologies:* Go to Settings > Accessibility > VoiceOver > Web, then turn on Accessibility Events. This setting may reveal whether an assistive technology is active on your iPad.

Tip: If you pair Magic Keyboard with iPad, you can use single-key Quick Nav commands to navigate webpages.

Read math equations using VoiceOver

VoiceOver can read math equations on the web (encoded using MathML) and in supported Apple apps such as Numbers and Keynote.

- *Hear an equation:* Have VoiceOver read the text as usual. VoiceOver says "math" before it starts reading an equation.

- *Explore the equation:* Double-tap the selected equation to display it in full screen and move through it one element at a time. Swipe left or right to read elements of the equation. Use the rotor to select Symbols, Small Expressions, Medium Expressions, or Large Expressions, then swipe up or down to hear the next element of that size. You can continue to double-tap the selected element to "drill down" into the equation to focus on the selected element, then swipe left or right, or up or down, to read one part at a time.

Equations spoken by VoiceOver can also be output to a braille device using Nemeth code, as well as the codes used by Unified English Braille, British English, French, and Greek.

Navigate in Maps with VoiceOver

In the Maps app, you can use VoiceOver to explore a region, browse points of interest, follow roads, zoom in or out, select a pin, or get information about a location.

- *Control how the map tracks your current location:* Double-tap ➶ until you hear the tracking option you want:

  - *Tracking on:* The map automatically centers on your current location.

  - *Tracking on with heading:* The map automatically centers on your current location and rotates so that the heading you're facing is at the top of the screen. In this mode, iPad speaks street names and points of interest as you approach them.

  - *Tracking off:* The map doesn't automatically center on your current location.

  Explore the map: Drag your finger around the screen, or swipe left or right to move to another item.

  Zoom in or out: Select the map, set the rotor to Zoom, then swipe down or up with one finger.

Pan the map: Swipe with three fingers.

Browse visible points of interest: Set the rotor to Points of Interest, then swipe up or down with one finger.

Follow a road: Hold your finger down on the road, wait until you hear "pause to follow," then move your finger along the road while listening to the guide tone. The pitch increases when you stray from the road.

Select a pin: Touch a pin, or swipe left or right to select the pin.

Get information about a location: With a pin selected, double-tap to display the information flag. Swipe left or right to select the More Info button, then double-tap to display the information page.

Use Camera, Photos, and Voice Memos with VoiceOver

Use VoiceOver gestures to take and edit Camera videos and Voice Memo recordings.

- *Pause or continue a recording:* Double-tap the screen with two fingers.

- *Trim a video:* While viewing a video in Photos, double-tap the screen to display the video controls, then select the beginning or end of the trim tool. Then swipe up to drag to the right, or swipe down to drag to the left. VoiceOver announces the amount of time the current position will trim from the recording. To complete the trim, select Trim, then double-tap.

- *Trim a voice memo:* Select the memo in Voice Memos, tap Edit, then tap Start Trimming. Select the beginning or end of the selection, double-tap and hold, then drag to adjust. VoiceOver announces the amount of time the current position will trim from the recording. Tap Play to preview the trimmed recording. When you've got it the way you want it, tap Trim.

How to Stop iPhone and iPad Apps From Updating Automatically

By default, apps on your iPhone or iPad will update automatically overnight when they're connected to power and a Wi-Fi network. It's a really useful feature if you're the kind of person who always wants to use the latest version of the apps. But the way that some app updates move, this can be a double-edged sword.

You wake up one day and you find out that your favorite image editor (like Snapseed) has redesigned its entire interface. And what if you don't like the new design? Because this is iOS, there is no simple way to roll back an app update. If you've been burned by a similar experience before, it's time to turn off automatic updates for good. Go back to manually updating apps and get the control back in your life.

How to Stop Automatic App Updates on iPhone and iPad

Step 1: Open the Settings app on your iPhone or iPad.

Step 2: Tap on iTunes & App Store.

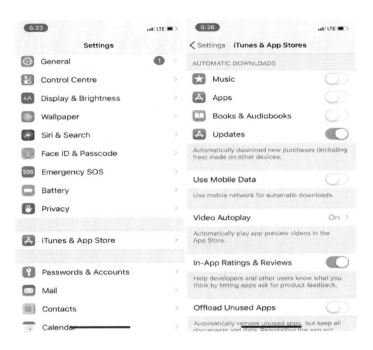

Step 3: From the Automatic Downloads section, find the Updates option and turn it off.

Now, none of the apps on your iPhone or iPad will update on its own. Let's take a look at home to updates apps the old style.

How to Manually Update Apps on iPhone and iPad

The fact that you've turned off automatic updates doesn't mean you're in the clear. You'll still have to update apps at some point. Apps like WhatsApp or

Messenger might stop working if you're not on the latest version. And for some apps and games like PUBG, you actively might be looking out for new updates.

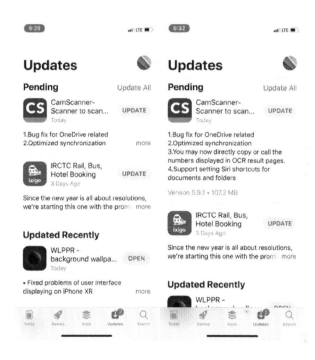

For this, there's the Updates tab in the App Store. Open the App Store app and tap on the Updates tab. Here you'll see a list of all the apps with available updates. You can take your time to read the app release notes to see what's new in the update. Tap on the More button to expand the release notes description.

When you've made sure that you do want to update an app, tap on the Update button. If you want to update all the apps listed in one fell swoop, tap on the Update All button.

Thank you for purchasing our user guide!

Index

H

I

L

M

N

P

Q

R

S

Printed in Great Britain
by Amazon

59353667R00147